RISING STARS
AND OZARK
CONSTELLATIONS

Best wishes,
Vicki Cox

RISING STARS AND OZARK CONSTELLATIONS

How did I find the Ozarks?
I looked for its constellations.
How did I find its constellations?
I connected the shining stars.

VICKI COX

photography by
Vicki Cox

SKYWARD PUBLISHING, INC.

DALLAS, TEXAS
www.skywardpublishing.com
skyward@sheltonbbs.com

Copyright 2001 by Skyward Publishing, Inc.

Publisher: Skyward Publishing, Inc
              Dallas, Texas
              Phone/Fax (573) 717-1040
              E-Mail: skyward@sheltonbbs.com
              Web Site: www.skywardpublishing.com

Library of Congress Cataloging-in-Publication Data

Cox, Vicki, 1945-
    Rising stars and Ozark constellations: faces of courage, ingenuity, and success/Vicki Cox; photography by Vicki Cox..
        p. cm.
      Includes bibliographical references (p. 292) and index.
        ISBN 1-881554-07-4
1. Ozark Mountains Region--Social life and customs.
2. Ozark Mountains Region--Biography.
3. Ozark Mountains Region--History, Local. 1. Title.

F417.09.C69 2000

                                CIP
976.7'1--dc21   OO-O38787

Cover and book design by
Angela Underwood
www.booksindesign.com

ATTENTION SCHOOLS AND CORPORATIONS

Skyward Publishing books are available at quantity
discounts with bulk purchase for educational,
business, or sales promotional use. For information
write to:

Skyward Publishing, Inc.
Marketing
813 Michael Street
Kennett, Missouri 63857
(573) 717-1040
E-mail: skyward@sheltonbbs.com

To my parents,
Marie and Hiram Jenkins,
whose spirits have always
lit my way.

THE
MISSOURI
OZARKS

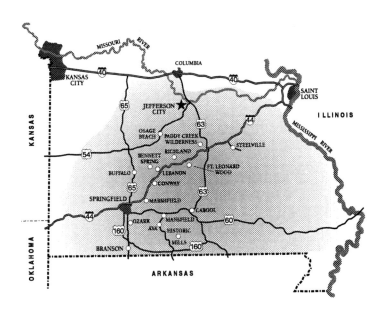

Table of Contents

Foreword

Defining the Ozarks is like finding the sky. I knew where to look; I just didn't know when I got there.

Certainly the Ozark character is connected with the land. The Ozark Plateau rose up in one majestic piece to claim sovereignty over the Midwest. No volcanic upheaval, spewing in undignified display created its hills. No glacier gouged out its valleys. Instead, its own streams, creeks, and rivers wore down the earth from within until the hills wreathed the region like garlands. Having created itself, the Plateau sustains itself. No mountain snow from higher elevations, or soil, settling as silt from other lands, gives it life. Springs, bubbling from cracks in the rocks, replenish its waters. Man's concrete constructions are just momentary intrusions its indifference temporarily allows. For eventually, the Ozarks reasserts itself. The bruising of industry and commerce's rude irreverence will disappear into the undergrowth as if a dowager queen merely rearranged the folds of her emerald robe.

Obviously, the present Ozark personality connects with pioneer forefathers. They survived in a difficult environment by looking within. They endured, like the land, because they were sufficient of themselves. Though much has been made of the region's stiff-backed independence, this proud heritage is not entirely the essence of the Ozarks. Other isolated hill and mountain cultures developed this trait as well.

None of this, however, concerned me when I visited

Branson, Gainesville, Mansfield, Springfield, Cabool, Conway, Marshfield, Buffalo, and Bennett Spring to write my features. I gave no thought to it as I explored Lebanon, Richland, Fort Leonard Wood, traveling to the Plateau's borders, west to Kansas City or north to Jefferson City.

The country-music star, cake baker, educator, author, musket maker, veterinarian, rock collector, fisherman, newscaster, jazz lover, and the judge who live in these locations possessed another quality that intrigued my editors and me. The people I have interviewed have looked within themselves, discovered who they are, and have liked what they've found. That acceptance validates their work and their pleasures. Without aspirations or pretensions beyond themselves, they simply go about living their lives, unaffected by the whims of convention or the fluctuations of popularity.

The Ozark persona is not a birthright. Not every person born within the Ozark geography inherits it. Nor is everyone outside the Ozarks bereft of it. But those who live here—and are recognized as genuine Ozarkers—possess this self-validation. Free from the constrictions of custom, true Ozarkers, in pleasing themselves, accomplish the extraordinary and the unusual. Sometimes they achieve national prominence because of it. Wanting to sing, the Mabe brothers stepped on stage barefoot and stamped the pattern for Branson's neon today. Combining summer fun with lessons for the spirit, "Spike" and Darnell White created a children's sports camp that develops the body and the soul. Recording her life for her daughter, Laura Ingalls Wilder became "Half Pint" to the entire world. Hale Fireworks sparklers, a part-time job, and Charlie Reading's fly rods, an after-hours passion, grew to reputations respected throughout the country. LeRoy Walls, Ruth Massey, Terri Bitting and Char Fox found their destiny and receive acclaim for it.

From every corner of the region, the bright Ozark lights drew me to them. They've radiated from a courtroom crowded with history and from a solitary study where books are written that have not yet sold. They've glowed from a greenhouse where miniature plants are grown for the simple pleasure of shaping a leaf and from a steamy kitchen where the clarity of apple jelly is more precious than faceted jewels. They've shone from a football field where the star quarterback plays her flute in the morning and then runs a power sweep to the left on Saturday afternoon. They've come from a makeshift barn lot where horses' hooves pound manure and broken hay into a dust so thick I could hardly breathe. They've lured me down the smooth interstate and over paths so old the gravel cracked.

What connects the men and women, children and adults, in this anthology is the Ozark self-reliance, self-awareness, and self-acceptance, drawn like straight lines, from dot-to-dot.

How did I find the Ozarks? I looked for its constellations. How did I find its constellations? I connected the shining stars.

The
Lights of
BRANSON

The First Family of Country Western Shows

The Baldknobbers Jamboree

I f Branson has an imprint, the Baldknobbers Jamboree put it there. The five dozen shows crowding the curbs in the Music Show Capital retrace the pattern made by the Mabe family fun over forty years ago. Though now all gussied

up in glitter and amplified by sound systems that shatter glass, the design they created has "family" stamped all over it. Entertainment along Route 76 lights up around America's music, sectioned into gospel, bluegrass, patriotic, rock and

The four Mabe brothers of the Baldknobbers, left to right: Jim "Droopy Drawers," Bill, Lyle "George Aggernite," and Bob. "Back then kids would say, 'We want to see a hillbilly.' We gave them a whole stage full of hillbillies," says Bill Mabe. (Photo courtesy of Baldknobbers Jamboree.)

roll, and classic country. Wedged between, like frets on a steel guitar, are hillbilly comedians, mouthing jokes straight out of corn pone and the backyard outhouse. The evening is split by an intermission just long enough to buy souvenirs and catch musicians' autographs at the stage apron.

This tradition is so deeply etched into vacationers' psyches that Branson is the nation's number one motor-coach destination and among the top five by car. The teenager slouched in row twenty, the young couple with toddlers in tow, and the sweat-shirted seniors have all crisscrossed the country to experience it.

Who'd have thought things would have become so psychological or technological when Bill, Jim, Lyle, and Bob Mabe took off their shoes and snapped on their overalls Friday and Saturday nights in downtown Branson in 1959. As Wee-Willie, Droopy Drawers, George Aggernight, and Bob-A-Link, they were just having a good time with washboard, tub bass, banjo, dobro and corny jokes. They hoped their weekend hobby would grow to full-time musical careers. The idea was a natural. They'd cut their teeth on the treble clef, playing at funerals, pie suppers, and fox hunts as youngsters in Highlandville. For a time, they performed live music on radio station KWTO in Springfield.

"We thought we'd start a little music show. We didn't mean for it to do anything," said Bill Mabe, founder and co-owner of the present-day Baldknobbers dynasty. "We were just having fun. Some people say now, 'You're making fun of hillbillies.' We didn't have any intentions of that at all. We were the hillbillies. That's what the whole area was about. Back then, kids would say, 'We want to see a hillbilly.' Well, we gave them a whole stage full of hillbillies. We just played and sang and established the show."

The Baldknobbers Hillbilly Jamboree Stage Show was a family venture. The wives packed sandwiches for their men to grab en route from their day jobs at the Hagman Candy Company. Joyce and Katie, Bill and Jim's wives, worked the street wearing "Show This Way" signboards and tried to convince at least fifteen people to walk up the stairs of city hall and sit among the folding chairs. They sold tickets to "big'uns" for a dollar; "little'uns" paid fifty cents. All dolled up in full-length organza, they started the merchandise industry that hovers beside today's shows. The tee-shirted teddy bears for autographing, baseball hats, CDs, and cassettes harken back to 1959 when the women sold black and white photos for mementos of a hillbilly vacation near Lake Taneycomo.

Bill said eight years passed between the Baldknobbers' first efforts and the emergence of other regional family-style country shows. The Presleys' Mountain Music Jubilee set up in 1967, and that show was followed by The Foggy River Boys, the Plummer Family, and some twenty others.

Building the Branson persona was a joint effort among entrepreneurs. The area's biggest draw was the Ozark village crafts at Silver Dollar City. The Baldknobbers performed as the first street band and staged gunfights in outdoor skits. Down the road, they were the hooded vigilantes in the *Shepherd of the Hills Pageant*. In return they advertised their own show.

"We used to know each other," recalled Bill of the area's early development. "We all used to work together and help each other out."

Ironically, the Baldknobbers started the influx of big-name celebrities. Having outgrown city hall, the Sammy Lane Pavilion, and the local skating rink, the Baldknobbers moved to their own theater on "The Strip."

"We started that," admitted Bill of the performing palaces that now break the skyline between motels, miniature golf courses, antique stores, and water slides. "We used to begin the season with a Nashville star. They'd come in for the season's opening. They'd have an afternoon and night show; then we'd play," said Bill.

When Barbara Mandrell, Dolly Parton, Mel Tellis, and Ernest Tubb looked across the Baldknobbers' footlights and found that six million vacationers dropped by for summer good times, the move was on. Today, Bobby Vinton's Blue Velvet Theater, the Andy Williams' Moon River logo, Kenny Roger's Branson Belle Showboat, and the Grand Palace's antebellum columns landmark the area as much as Harold Bell Wright's log cabin or Marvel Cave.

"I can remember when they first came in. We got pretty scared," Bill said of the big-name entertainers. "But everyone who comes in seems to help our crowds. We end up with some of the crowds anyway," Mabe said.

Having a national reputation doesn't always guarantee a Branson success. Tourist centers are littered with brochures of stars who shimmered briefly and then burned out. Those who survive may credit their success to what takes place inside the Baldknobbers' seventeen-hundred seat auditorium.

"They've slipped in the back doors to see what has to be done to stay down here," said Mabe. "They discover you can't sit on a stool and just sing for two hours."

The Baldknobbers' longevity may result from their ability to spruce up their original format for generations entertained by both The Grand Ole Opry and MTV. An evening at the Baldknobbers Jubilee is a fast-paced production, wrapping the traditional fifties formula in an up-tempo package. It seduces both the eye and the ear; it tickles the funny bone and touches the heart.

"We get a lot more sophisticated audience now," he said. "Right at first it had to be pretty country to come to our show. But it's not that way now; there's so many types of shows down here."

Joyce agreed. "You have to change with the times. You just can't sit still and let everything change around you. You have to grow with it."

Though all of the original brothers have retired, the organization is steeped in Mabe second and third generation kinfolk. Dennis (Bill and Joyce's son) is featured male soloist. Joy Bilyeu, Bill's granddaughter, lends her full, rich voice to female features. Brent, Lyle's son, plays bass. Tim picked up the hillbilly hat his dad as "Droopy Drawers" retired.

Music at the Baldknobbers is star. The eighteen-person ensemble round robins through the twenty-song repertoire. It moves nonstop through "Fever," "Won't You Give Me Just One More Chance?" and "Tumblin' Tumbleweeds."

"It's just a good variety," said Joyce. "If you're not wild about something that's going on, wait a minute and there'll be something else. It just clicks."

"Music has come a long way from the fifties," Bill recalled. "At first we did hillbilly songs like "She'll Be Coming 'Round the Mountain," or "Rollin' in My Sweet Baby's Arms." Then we did country. If you got out of three chords, that was something. Now it's progressed way past three chords. Now it's cool country, like Reba or Faith Hill."

As musical producer, Bill oversees multiple arrangements such as the technical, the musical, and the costume rehearsals their complex production numbers require. Lighting complements the lyrics; environmental haze enhances spotlights.

"We used to play a song one time," Bill said. "Today the band gets their arrangement, the singers get theirs, and then we add choreography. Sometimes we'll work all day just to get through one song."

Choice of costumes for a Baldknobbers' show is hardly subliminal. Joyce supervises a wardrobe that has progressed from the red gingham to denim to inset leather. "Back then, women never thought about what we'd see on stage," she recalled. "They might have two changes: one for the first half, one for the second. Today, we try to match each costume to the song they are singing."

Through eleven costume changes, Joy, Kelly Van Hoose, and Chris Gentile are draped in purple and six-inch fringe or suede turquoise or debutante chiffon. They dance in knee-high go-go boots or clog in square-dance crinolines. The black leather leggings demand as much attention as their close-harmony yodeling.

Branson keeps considering new ways to make the most of the tourist's days. Jennifer Wilson and others perform mornings, some with breakfast. Two dozen now offer matinees. Taneycomo's tinsel town burns the neon from March until Ozark Mountain Christmas closes the season in mid-December. Mabe supports a yearlong season but opposes allowing gambling in the town he helped to build. "It would ruin our image," he said. "Branson got its name as a family-oriented area. We hope to keep it that way."

With the restaurant and motel under Jim's direction, Bill

and Joyce arrive at the theater before the ragtime warm-up begins. Bill critiques from the shadows while Joyce reads upstairs.

"It's just our life. We've done it all these years," she explained of their nightly trip from Nixa. Bill just laughs. "What I'm doing was my hobby. It became my job, and now it's too late to find another hobby."

The Baldknobbers Jamboree may end up more famous than the vigilantes they were named after. The original gang just took justice. In Branson, where the audience is a treasure and applause is gold, the Mabe family has stolen the show.

Yankee Doodle Girl
Jennifer Wilson

Million dollar legs stretch from her four-inch heels to a demure derriere. A coast-to-coast smile and topknot of blonde curls finish the picture. No caption's needed: Betty Grable, All-American pin-up poster girl.

Or is it? Although that over-the-shoulder face is familiar, it is better recognized on Branson's billboards. Jennifer Wilson's meticulous reproduction of the World War II classic is yet another streamer in the red-white-and-blue banner that unfurls about her.

Named as the worldwide spokesperson for the USO in 1996, the Branson entertainer draped the bunting of country, God, and family across the world just as troops headed toward Bosnia. Jennifer's first extended tour for U.S. servicemen abroad was a twenty-

(Photo courtesy of Jennnifer Wilson)

eight day circuit in Europe. Certain only of its uncertainty, she prepared for any circumstances: auditorium, aircraft carrier, a flatbed truck, musicians, or track music.

"You never know what may come up. You just have to be ready for anything," Jennifer said. "Wherever the troops are going or if war breaks out, I'm on call. The USO is about bringing people a little touch of home."

To be prepared, Jennifer packed a full trunk of entertainment: country music, comedy, jazz dances, sweet ballads, and costumes, all showing lots of leg. The USO organization did not format her show or advise her. Neither did Bob Hope, whom she met briefly when he visited Branson.

"He was the perfect gentlemen," she recalled of the only other person who shares her USO title. "He was very sweet to me. He said, 'Ah, the USO's doing pretty good, aren't they?'"

As USO entertainer, Jennifer has distributed her musical and verbal CARE packages closer to home. Flown to the Hines Veterans Hospital in Chicago, she's spent four hours visiting with the servicemen in the spinal unit there. "It was hard," she recalled of her Veteran's Day duties. "They were in such bad condition; many were bedridden. Many were young, recently wounded. We went to cheer them up, talk, and let them know we loved them. Mostly they just seem to want to know you love and respect them."

She's also sung the national anthem in Dallas, Texas, at a USO dinner for former President George Bush and his wife, Barbara, and unveiled a memorial at the Branson Meadow development. She's been awarded the "Silver Helmet Award for Americanism" from the AM VETS National Honors and Awards Committee. Sandwiched between performing the national anthem and "God Bless America," she learned of her

USO title while at the Freedom Flight America Convention of World War II veterans. "They were on to me that I was the right type and age and attitude," Jennifer said of her USO recognition. "I'm easy to talk to; I'm very family-oriented myself and warm. That's something you need when you're bringing a bit of home to them."

Being a hometown girl comes easily to Jennifer. She grew up between the tiny towns of Moberly and Huntsville, Missouri. "They argue over me," she said. "I went to school in Huntsville, but my mailing address is Moberly."

Her father owned an electrical and plumbing business; her mother, a full-time homemaker, helped him with the books. Her dad played a little guitar; her mother once studied dance.

But it takes steel as well as rhinestones to tap out a career on the stage, and her parents' high expectations tempered Jennifer's dream to dance. "Melanie, my middle sister, and I put together little shows. She would chord and pick a little bit. I wanted to sing and dance, push to the front, and do the flashy stuff. My parents would tell me, 'Have your act together. Don't get up there and fumble around. Go practice, and then we sure would like to be invited to see you.'"

Besides putting together shows for the family, the girls performed at school assemblies and other organizations. "Once we did "Grand Ol' Flag," she recalled. "We really nailed it too."

By age sixteen Jennifer had her own dance studio, "Jennifer's All That Jazz," a business she maintained for ten years.

Jennifer may have been high stepping to the music, but her feet were squarely on the ground when she attended

Stephens College. She carried a triple load, graduating with a Bachelor of Arts degrees in dance and the humanities as well as a minor in psychology.

"My dad told me, "You can take classes in anything as long as you do it well. You will do something with what I'm giving you. You will give it a hundred percent.' So when I hit college, I was all business. Those little things follow you.'"

Jennifer then studied ballet in San Antonio, returning to the University of Missouri for graduate studies. Within a year, she completed her master's degree in educational and counseling psychology. While maintaining her dance studio, she observed dance's therapeutic benefits.

"I've seen children in the studio go from the most shy and inhibited to the most outgoing and exuberant just because they moved and began to communicate. I did a lot of positive reinforcement there."

She pursued both her psychology and dance, performing part-time and working with behavior-disordered children in the Moberly Junior High.

"They started out the loudest and ended up the best-behaved students in the school," said Jennifer. "They had tremendous spirit. We just rechanneled their energies. It sure does change people's success rate when they start looking with a positive attitude."

Jennifer next helped the chronically ill in the outpatient ward of Kirksville Osteopathic Hospital. Her caseload included manic-depressives and schizophrenics who were preparing to leave their institutionalized environment.

"I worked there three years—which was my goal," she said. "I wanted to know the things I learned in my master's for sure—in my bones, not just in my mind."

Juggling her vocation and weekend performances at the Salt River Opry made her restless. "I had been praying about it for more than six months. I wasn't totally happy."

Her big break came in a guest audition on the Tony James' That's Show Biz Talent Show in Branson where she was seen by romance novelist, Janet Dailey and her husband, Bill. Taken by her singing and dancing abilities, Bill became her manager. "He saw I was very ambitious," said Jennifer, "and that I needed to be promoted."

She credits Dailey's ideas for cranking up the wattage on the early-morning marquees. Though four other shows were trying to lure audiences away from souvenir shopping, it was "Jennifer in the Morning" that turned the spotlights and advertising on full force. As a result, there are nearly two dozen morning shows for tourist to choose from, and Jennifer has herself moved twice before settling in her own Americana Theater.

"He broke the market on it," Jennifer said of Dailey. "He put up the billboards. Now it's a full scale nighttime show in the morning."

Dailey also created the 1994 "Christmas Gift from Branson" telecast that brought Jennifer to the attention of the USO organization. With John Davidson, she co-hosted the ninety-minute variety show that aired on the Armed Forces Radio and Television Network. Including guest appearances of servicemen's mothers and a Christmas tree full of ornaments with servicemen's names, the show was broadcast three times to over three hundred stations and to two hundred million listeners. The show has had repeat performances.

"He put it all together as a gift of time and talent for the military," said Jennifer. "There was such a tremendous community support for it since everything in Branson is based on God, family and country."

Jennifer's variety show develops around her singing and dancing, with generous flashes of long legs and eyelashes. To the glitz, she adds patriotic, comedy, and gospel segments. "Of course, I witness on stage and give a brief testimony. I'm proud to say I'm a born-again Christian. When I moved to Branson, it was just like coming home."

In tribute to her down-home roots, Jennifer's mother, Peggy, wrote "He'll Lift Me Up," the title song for Jennifer's 1995 album. Peggy plans to write other songs for her daughter's future albums.

Jennifer's career after the program and other service-related projects began marching to its own cadence. The idea for the pin-up pose developed from comments made by veterans who were in the audience. "People kept telling me, 'You have the prettiest legs—just like Betty Grable's.' Then Bill came up with the idea to duplicate the photo." Replicating the original Betty Grable's shadows, position of the charms on the bracelet, and tendrils of the hair required a four-hour photo session.

"There's a lot about us that are alike," said Jennifer of the 1940 star of "Follow the Fleet," "Pin-Up Girl," and "A Yank in the RAF." "She was from Missouri; she acted and sang and danced. She was really down to earth. I'm about as down to earth as you can get."

Savvy enough to know a dancing career has its limits, Jennifer has plans for another partnership with her sister in the future. Once out of the spotlight, Jennifer says she will return to her psychology training. With Melanie as principal, the two will organize a Christian school. "First I want to entertain," she said. "Then I want to help troubled children."

Until then, Jennifer remains on her toes. Besides USO touring, she puts together a new show for the two hundred fifty-five performances she gives during a season. In between rehearsing, choreographing and costuming hunts, she models, visits friends, and answers fan mail.

"I like to do it myself. They wrote me the letter. If they open up their heart to me, the least I can do is write back. I like what I do," said Jennifer Wilson. "I'm one of the happiest people I know. I've worked a long time to get where I am. I thank the Lord every day. Once He gets the people here, it's my job to entertain them."

The USO has chosen well. If flags could have rhinestones, Jennifer Wilson's smile could put them there. Jennifer Wilson is a Yankee Doodle Dandy from her Betty Grable legs to her Midwestern past.

Breathing God's Good Air
Spike and
Darnell White

"Spike" and Darnell White are co-authors of a book on grandparenting, I Need You. For three decades the couple has headed Kamp Kanakuk, a summer experience for teens, which combines athletics and spiritual growth.

Was it pixie dust or children's laughter that sprinkled Spike and Darnell White with youth? Either is possible. Their world's been landscaped by Indian teepees and cabins trimmed with childhood's yellow, red, and blue. The tallest things on their horizon, next to the Ozark

Mountains, are the water slides and fiber flumes that curl down Kanakuk Kamp's slopes toward Lake Taneycomo in Branson.

Only numbers can convince anyone that these two are eight decades in age. Their outward appearance certainly gives no hint. They move too easily. They work too hard. They think too quickly. They've been married six decades, raised three sons, love eight grandchildren, and sit atop an organization that touches fourteen thousand children every summer. They've spent a lifetime creating good times for the young.

Spike always credits his success to Darnell. "Be sure, be sure, be sure to marry the right woman. After that, it's downhill all the way. We've been a team," he said, smiling toward his wife. "It sure is fun."

Her quick grin validates the "fun" and "team" in his tribute. "It's been a team deal. We've been so blessed," said Darnell. "The key is respect for the other's interests."

Just as their talk dovetails into a single conversation, they've written alternate chapters in I Need You (Questar Publishers) a scrapbook of their experiences as grandparents. When Spike suggests that grandparents and grandchildren should share travel adventures, it's because he's done it. Advising that grandparents' homes should be full of "kid corners," he's describing their own house. He credits his "best friend" and "sweetheart" for providing the porch swing, dress-up clothes, and songbooks on the piano for grandchildren's play. When Darnell mentions descriptive, intricate letters, it's because she's at the computer, composing the epic family newsletter herself.

Advice in I Need You snaps together like Legos out of the

toy box. Be a good example. Be positive. Be involved. Be attentive. Be available. Be enjoyable. Effective grandparenting, according to the Whites, begins with a healthy, active, interesting person.

"I'd rather see a good testimony than hear one," Spike said from his arsenal of one-liners. Darnell concurred. She writes that living examples are critical in a child's life.

"That role means teaching and inspiring and being— who we are, where we are, how we are, and when we are."

The Whites practice what they preach. Their talk is liberally punctuated with projects to complete or interests to explore. Their home is decorated with mementos from trips to China and Africa and with snapshots of kayaking with grandsons Lance, Wesley, and Scott down the Colorado and Rio Grande rivers.

"I outlived all my canoe partners," said Spike of the hobby he began in his seventies, "so I started kayaking."

Trim in black jeans and pageboy hairstyle, Darnell's appearance belies a birth year marking the ending of a World War. Her daily routine includes a two-mile walk on the treadmill. "I used to jog," she admitted, "but then I slowed to walking. The grandkids now ask, 'Grandma, have you been woggin' lately?'" She rises at 6 a.m. to water the flowers around the chapel and tend her squash plants. She and son, Joe, compete at growing gourds.

"I said, 'I'm going to make this fun. Let's see who has the longest gourd and the longest vine by the end of camp,'" she explained.

Heading to her office, a glassed-in cabin a few steps from home, she tackles the computer and paperwork of the Kanakuk organization.

"I work every day. I do all the government forms, check payroll, and reconcile the balances. I do my work well; I've done it for so long," she said.

With Joe behind the corporate desk, Spike buzzes about in his red pick-up, keeping his finger on camp operations. He oversees pouring concrete, visits with maintenance about the chlorinating system, or suggests that the flagpoles are a washer-width off plumb. Gulping down a mouthful of Mountain Dew and a Snickers bar, he heads out for a "God-Don't-Make-No-Junk" talk with campers. When summer ends, he supervises construction projects.

"What's the use of just hanging around," Spike said, disdaining retirement. Darnell just shakes her head. "Spike is always busy," she said. "He wears out his clothes from the inside."

If inspiring by example is the foundation of the White family, it is the cornerstone of Kanakuk Kamp. As Darnell quietly acknowledges, "We are the camp." The Whites' life work swings on the strong Christian witness of top-athlete counselors. In a one-to-four ratio, young university students spend sixteen hours a day with the youngsters in an intense sports environment.

"It's a different kind of ministry," Spike said. "Every kid we can crowd in is exposed to Christ through athletics. Kids hear a Christian testimony from a six foot nine-inch basketball player who stuffs basketballs with both hands or a three-hundred pound football player who says, 'Jesus is the answer.'"

The philosophy has prospered. Spike's only partially kidding when he jokes that he remembers campers' fathers or grandfathers. A half century ago, Spike was a seventeen-year-

In a one-to-four ratio, young university students spend sixteen hours a day with the young-sters in an intense sports environment. (Photo courtesy of Kamp Kanakuk)

old junior counselor directing fifteen boats and a fleet of five canoes around the lake. Today seven camp locations spill in every direction, with rope swings, swimming pools, basketball courts, archery targets, gymnastics apparatus, and soccer fields. Children, ages seven to seventeen, unload from June through August. A staff of fifteen hundred greets them. Two camps for inner-city youth and another for the handicapped or kids with cancer operate under the not-for-profit I'm Third Foundation. The Whites designated proceeds from *I Need You* to the foundation.

As entrepreneurs, as grandparents, and as individuals, the Whites have created a merry-go-round-life that is lit by one word. "Fun," said Spike. "I've been blessed with fun."

The good humor within Darnell and Spike and between them is infectious. Spike will tease anyone: his wife, a staff member, or a camper. Not surprisingly, they tease him back. On the one-lane paths winding through the camp's sporting complex, Spike maneuvers through campers' affectionate greetings, mostly yelled from bunk beds and front porch steps. Those close enough to stop the truck hope to trade good-natured insults with the grandfather of all campers.

Both Whites encourage grandparents to develop fun with their grandchildren. Fittingly, their grandchildren write a section in *I*

Need You. They list the good times the Whites concocted for them. Jamie Jo writes of tea parties, building snowmen, cleaning the pond, and jumping in the leaves. Wesley remembers Darnell's Christmas game of hiding presents and Easter egg hunts on Whippoorwill Hill. Scott recalls kayaking at Nantahala Outdoor Center, coon hunting, and bow hunting with Spike. Cody tells how Darnell took him fishing and baited his hook, played pool, and shot hoops at camp with him.

Ultimately, *I Need You* reveals that the most important value in a grandparent's treasure chest is the gift of time. Being an interesting, energetic person enhances the grandparent/ grandchild relationship. Fun activities set the stage for that relationship. However, the White grandchildren see right to the real issue. Darnell and Spike push aside business schedules to be a presence in their lives. They have listened to problems and watched from the edge of the basketball court or the band concert. The kids notice Darnell's efforts when she spends time researching an Indian costume for them or when she helps them through strep throat. They're keenly aware of her unhurried walk in the woods or her unruffled stride when they visit a college dorm.

Scott writes: *Other grandparents I know give their grandchildren all kinds of stuff, and then that's all the grandchild expects from the grandparent—just gifts. I think you should give them time, and that's what Spike and Darnell give to us a lot.*

The activities that grandparents provide for children naturally depend on the child's age and the family's economic circumstances. Good times can follow the wake of a sailboat, johnboat, yacht, or canoe. What the Whites' book said in its two hundred ten pages has nothing to do with money.

Grandchildren need a strong, vital, encouraging presence. They need to enjoy their elders. They need a grandparent whose actions speak louder than words. The message should be clear: *You are so important that I give you my most value possession, time.* Spike and Darnell White have done just that.

Souvenirs from the Ozark Woods
Walnut Bowls

Walnut bowls. Nothing's more ingrained in the tourist mind as the definitive Ozark souvenir. These sleek slant-sided containers have long graced dinner tables because of Shepherd Hills Walnut Bowls stores. For twenty-five years, the family-owned corporation

"When you go to Hawaii, you bring back a pineapple; at Disney World, you buy a Mickey Mouse hat. When you come to the Ozarks, you should take back a walnut bowl. It truly is a souvenir," said Rod Reid.

has wooed tourists off interstates in five states with its nearly perfect vacation artifact. Its three Missouri stores circle the high traffic areas of Branson, Osage Beach, and Lebanon.

"We essentially created the walnut bowl market. They're such a unique product," said Rod Reid. "In the beginning, we saw our customers once every five years. They wanted a memento of their one long, family vacation. Since Missouri grows more walnut than all the other states put together, walnut bowls were a natural."

Reid was hardly more than a sprout himself when his parents opened their first gift shop beside Interstate 44 at Lebanon's Exit 127. Hoping to finance their children's college education, Ida and Rea stocked the mom-and-pop operation with the usual bobbing-head ducks and snowflake paperweights.

"Mom noticed customers were more interested in walnut bowls than the other souvenirs, so that's the direction we went," said Reid.

Cut from Missouri bottomland, walnut wood was routinely shipped to Billings and Ozark manufacturers. Most of their bowls were destined for upscale department stores on both coasts. The Reids asked for "seconds," culled for sanding abrasions, wobbly glue lines or color variations. By marketing the minutely flawed, their Shepherd Hills business developed as one of the country's first of fifty factory outlets.

"My personal favorite is the bird-peck hole," said Reid. "To get a worm, the woodpecker drills a pin hole. Water gets in and makes a little dark spot. It doesn't affect usefulness, but in walnut bowl circles, it's considered a flaw."

While at the University of Missouri, Rod and his brother, Randy, rode the bus home weekends to help at the store. Intrigued by the black gold of Missouri's walnut trade, Rod abandoned his petroleum engineering major for accounting. Learning business management from the ground up, Rod drove the hundred thirty mile trip to the bowl manufacturers to restock the shelves.

The Reids learned life beside the fast lane needed blink-of-the-eye advertising. The twenty-five thousand tourists driving by each day rarely stopped long enough to buy newspapers. Radio messages required giving directions to listeners who could have already passed by the exits. The solution was billboard advertising. Their trademark red and orange signs announce, "Walnut Bowls," "Factory Seconds," "Half Price."

"In 1972 we had just one; a few people come in. Then we added four more; more people came in. Even today, we communicate with our customers primarily with billboards," said Reid.

Fifty presently line the roads, showing up fifty miles in any direction from each of the Reids' Missouri stores. Another forty signs circle their four locations in Tennessee, Illinois, Nebraska, and Kentucky. Over two decades, the Reids have seen the gauntlet of corncob pipes and state plate shops disappear, businesses that were replaced by clusters of outlet malls near tourist attractions. *The Wall Street Journal* revelation that shopping is the number one vacationer's activity is old news to the Reids.

"People shop to be entertained. They don't shop out of need. They want to get something that intrigues them and at a bargain price," said Reid. "Our business increased greatly because of the malls. Tourists once thought the Ozark region was a place where prices were inflated and many souvenirs were stamped with 'Made in Japan,'" said Reid. "Now people drive to Branson and Lake of the Ozarks just to shop for unique products and the bargains."

Walnut bowls still dominate merchandise found under

the Reids' roofs. Three sizes of serving and salad bowls, two-tiered candy dishes, and nut bowls stack eight deep on the best display case shelving. Recipe holders, serving utensils, and candleholders line up beside them.

As tourist travel patterns have changed, the Reids have diversified their business, branching out to include oak knick-knacks, housewares cutlery, Case pocketknives, pottery, greenery, and basketry. Reid said that though ninety percent of his customers live outside a hundred-mile radius, three-fourths are repeats shoppers to their counters.

"People are more mobile now," he explained. "If they plan a big cross-country trip, they fly. When they drive, it's for shorter, more frequent vacations from surrounding states. We may see the same customer four or five times a year. A set of walnut bowls lasts fifteen years."

Though Shepherd Hills Walnut Bowl stores are dependent on the tourist traffic, their peak days occur after travelers pack away summer shorts and tee shirts.

"The Columbus Day weekend is our busiest holiday of the year," said Reid. "It's a three-day weekend that sneaks up on people. They may go to Grandma's for Thanksgiving, Christmas, and the Fourth of July but not for Columbus Day. Besides the trees are turning, and everyone wants to get out and kick around."

The week after Christmas ends their high-volume traffic. "With gift money in their pocket, people hit the road one more time—either to head home from the holidays or to buy what they really want," Reid explained.

Stepping from the three hundred tour buses or the family car for a bargain and a clean bathroom, customers can leave the Reid staff either smiling or grimacing.

"It's not uncommon for our staff to be tipped. One woman gave our sales clerk fifty dollars. We get compliments every day about being friendly. That's something the Ozarks is known for.   But then, another lady tried to return a set of knives. Sure enough, she had her receipt, only it was dated 1986," said Reid. Although willing to accommodate most customer requests, the Reids declined to return her money. They sell seconds; they don't buy secondhand.

Overlooked by scavenger squirrels, fallen walnuts settle into the rocky Ozark soil and take root. Thirty years later, they become lettuce or fruit containers. Then by some nick of fate or scratch by time, they end up at Shepherd Hills Walnut Bowls. Still their beauty and their usefulness continue.

Ugly Ducklings Sit Pretty
on Land and Water
Ride the Ducks

It's a gaggle of geese—a covey of quail—a flock of birds. So what's a bunch of ducks? In Branson, the answer is success. Ride the Ducks Sightseeing Tours has been splashing into Table Rock Lake and looping Branson roads for

Begun as a little retirement business, McDowell family's Ride the Ducks Tours has grown into a full-time enterprise, serving Boston, Seattle and Branson. (Photo courtesy of Ride the Ducks)

three decades. Their wake even spreads to Boston's Charles River and the beaches of Clearwater, Florida, where tourists fill Ducks for excursions through eastern landmarks.

The vehicle, an ugly duckling of transportation, has outwardly changed little in fifty years. Aesthetic and aerodynamics were hardly considerations when the seven-ton box on wheels transported troops from ships to Normandy and Iwo Jima beach-heads. With their military missions ended after the war, many Ducks were dry-docked, abandoned to rust and rot in empty fields or surplus depots. Others, more fortunate, found a purpose in the tourist industry.

Ride the Ducks dipped into Branson's waters in 1971 when Dr. Lloyd Gillespie and Gary Snadon brought three units to the Ozark region. Six years later, the McDowells waded in. The land and water attraction set up shop at a fifteen-by-thirty-foot building on the side of Highway 76. It had one restroom but lacked a garage. Three thousand people rode between the five music shows to take a gander at cattle covering the hills.

"I didn't know anything about Ducks or how they operated," said Robert McDowell. "We enrolled in the school of hard knocks and learned as we went."

McDowell himself, two and a half years into a premed study in biology, simply intended to help his father, Jack McDowell, establish a retirement venture.

"He was finishing at Kraft, and I came down to refurbish the equipment. While I was rolling around in the gravel, I thought, 'Good grief, what an incentive to get back to school.' But we started giving tours, and I got hooked. When I wasn't covered with grease, I was in the library. I went to the vo-tech school three times a week to learn welding and wiring. I hung out at the machine shops and learned all I could."

Well past those early grimy days, McDowell no longer wears motor oil, and the Duck fleet is bigger than a flock. The ticket office and complex, though smaller than Wal-Mart behind it, is larger than the McDonald's restaurant next door. The Duck parking lot accommodates sixty buses. Ducks leave on the quarter hour and take seventy minutes to wind through the streets of

Branson, the Shepherd of the Hills Fish Hatchery, and Baird Mountain before plopping into Table Rock Lake. In a quarter of a century, two million have seen Branson sights from Duck viewpoint.

Besides introducing tourists to shows, tour guides discuss ways to get around in traffic, spill out a bit of Ozark humor and folk tales, and always pay a tribute to the military beginnings of the equipment. "Everyone truly enjoys going out in a Duck," said McDowell. "It's part of history. I've had some fellows who operated them at Normandy Beach share their experiences. You don't realize how life threatening it was to move in a vehicle running six miles per hour in the water. Very few got to shore. These Ducks carry more than passengers. They carry a lot of history."

McDowell's Ride the Duck business stays buoyant when lesser ventures sink like a rock because McDowell pays careful attention to detail. Like most amphibians, Ride the Ducks most important parts are either out of sight or under water. Before a driver slips behind the wheel to greet passengers, two tour coaches and local color experts who are knowledgeable in the community's history have prepared the person for the job.

"A lot of people assume if you go jump in the water, you have a tour," McDowell said. "Our drivers are well trained. They are a large part of who we are and what we do. We try to bring out all of the personality of the individual. Our philosophy is that we are doing customers a disservice if the drivers regurgitate a specific tour. We help them to create their own."

When the Ducks pull away from the main complex, they leave a wide support system rippling behind them. The building adjacent to the Duck terminal houses a technical side of Ride the Ducks that spreads through two levels of offices, training rooms, a garage, and a twenty-man staff. The maintenance shop partitions into welding, assembling, painting, and two warehouse areas.

The completeness of the Branson operation has brought partnerships to the Ducks from elsewhere. Though a dozen other operations splash around from Wisconsin to Key West, the success of Branson's Ride the Ducks had not gone unnoticed. In 1994 Andrew Wilson approached McDowell with the idea of bringing Ducks to Boston for sightseeing tours of Beacon Hill, Trinity Church, Harvard, and the Charles River.

McDowell has learned there is more to a tour than one might at first think. "You'd think it was the Boston Tea Party all over again," said McDowell in reference to the red tape and apprehensions the project stirred up. Assuming all the Ducks were vintage war variety, the city fathers feared a nightmare breakdown on roads where Paul Revere himself would have had trouble.

To solve the problem, McDowell merely put all his ducks in a row. He invited the bureaucratic skeptics to evaluate how his Ducks maneuvered on Ozark ridges. He wanted them to inspect the new edition Ducks he was manufacturing.

"What has set us apart in the industry is how we've improved the equipment," said McDowell. "This was apparent when the Public Department of Utilities came down. The only recommendation they had was for us to put a heat shield on the exhaust so no one would burn their hand."

The Duck tour has continued to grow in popularity. Trolley tours in Bean Town were often interrupted, even terminated, as people stepped on and off at whim. "There's such a huge resource of history that needs to be told. You can't get started telling the story of Boston in eighty minutes. But on a Duck you build the tour the whole way. You build up a relationship with the people.

You become a host for the city."

The Boston partnership won approval, and though getting through the political permit process cost it a partial season, Boston Duck tours have been in full swing since. Every tour is sold out.

"It has the potential to surpass us, if they are allowed to grow." McDowell said. The success of the Boston operation next caught the attention of Clearwater, Florida. Meticulous in his considerations, McDowell has developed what he calls a demographic evaluation to inquiries. "The first thing I ask concerns how much research have they done on this business," said McDowell. "Very few people know what they're getting into." Having met the qualifying criteria, the Clearwater company was invited to partner with the Branson corporation. Along with the Duck apparatus, they receive benefit of Branson Ducks' four-week training syllabus, maintenance schedules, tour route planning, marketing materials, and personnel training.

"There's not a lot of innovation out there," said McDowell of Duck design. "Elsewhere it's mainly patch it, put gas in it, and keep it running. But if you break down, you've got two hundred people climbing down your throat. We make sure they have bullet-proof equipment."

The Ride the Ducks future has never been in question. The only uncertainty is when McDowell can produce and market his new state-of-the-art Prototype Duck.

The vintage amphibian's specifications may have been all right for landing Normandy's beaches, but tourists, not soldiers, assault Branson. Rather than battleships, they arrive in motor coaches. Current Ducks require relegating the tour group into multiple vehicles, with some customers positioned outside the sun canopy on an elevated deck. ProtoDucks have been lengthened to accommodate the entire motor-coach population. Eliminating the step-up deck, it seats all customers on the same level, in the same direction, and under one sunroof.

McDowell can translate other improved technology and innovations with references to single-line brake systems, hull and dash-board configurations, updated undercarriages, and drive trains. But the bottom line is ProtoDuck is easier and safer for the driver and more convenient for the customer.

In the sophisticated world of Internet travel and virtual-reality entertainment, a business called Ride the Ducks seems a bit light in the tail feathers—not so for Robert McDowell. His affection for his fleet of gangly machinery is genuine.

"We have a lot of equity in Ride the Ducks," said McDowell. "When you say it, there's no question about what you're talking about. It' a name with a call to action."

Taking Off the White Gloves
Building a Library

L ittle 'ol ladies, the faint of heart, or social butterflies need not apply—not at the Taneyhills Library Club. Please come for conversation and good manners; listen to the music; admire the art. But know this. The white gloves do come off. There's a library to run.

Today two hundred Branson volunteers understand just that. And so did their foremothers, twenty-nine Presbyterian ladies in the Maids and Matrons Sunday School Class.

Bookended between 1933 and the present is the object of their devotion, the Taneyhills Community Library. Begun as a box of castoffs, the facility has grown to about 40,000 volumes. Now serving a population of 25,000 in Taney and Stone

Co-authors Kathleen Van Buskirk and Lorraine Humphrey pay tribute to the Taneyhills Library Club, who sustains the library with its jams and jellies, gentilities and guts.

counties, the library operates without a cent of tax money, sustained by the iron-will of Branson's women.

Written by Kathleen Van Buskirk and Lorraine Humphrey, *Bringing Books to the Ozarks* is a history of their tenacity. Against the background of Branson's development, this three hundred page book is a tribute the thousand volunteers whose jams and jellies, gentility and guts, have sustained the library.

"We started researching during the library's fiftieth anniversary," said Van Buskirk, a veteran journalist specializing in the Ozarks. "I didn't belong to the Library Club, but I read about their new building addition and got interested in its history. Since then, with me writing and Lorraine editing, the book's been a labor of love."

They found in old newspapers, purse-size yearbooks, and faded ledgers, a group of vital women who craved literary and intellectual discourse. Meet then Fanny Dawes who veneered the front of her house with rock, cared for her hemophiliac son, and suggested her fellow Presbyterians form the Taneyhills Study Club. Meet Pearl "Sparky" Spurlock who dressed in calico, sported a corncob pipe, and taxied tourists around Branson. Take a look at Rose O'Neill, addressing the Club in red velvet. Meet licensed embalmer, Minnie Whelchel, novelist Rose Wilder Lane, and concert violinist, Mona Neihardt. For a time the Study Club's monthly meetings centered on world affairs, current best sellers, and classical music, but that wasn't enough.

"These young women had to have something to study," said Van Buskirk. "They said, 'We can't afford new books, but we can pool the ones we've got.'"

Besides *Pollyanna* and *The Shepherd of the Hills*, the Study

Club members found one hundred fifty books to pass among themselves. On December 2, 1933, they made the books available to the general public, and the Taney County Public Library was born.

Their book collection, enlarged by donations from the community, newspaper reviewers, and other libraries, outgrew a garage, a front porch, and hotel pantry. It overfilled rented office space and rooms in Branson's community buildings. By 1977, it required a two-level freestanding structure and an addition that doubled its space eighteen years later.

As the library grew, so grew the responsibility for its care. The women in *Bringing Books to the Ozarks* meant business. "From the day Branson was started, women have been in business, either with their husbands or on their own, managing shops downtown," said Van Buskirk.

The restaurant resorts, hotels, drugstore, dress shop, and hat shop owners soon realized that a budget of $9.27 and nickel-and-dime dues could not support their project, so they used what they had available.

Early on, library workers compiled and printed a collection of poems by fellow member, poet and columnist, Mary Elizabeth Mahnkey. When, in 1941 *The Shepherd of the Hills* was made into a movie, they asked the book's publisher for distribution rights to the Harold Bell Wright classic. Though such on-going projects helped, solvency teetered so precariously on cash flow that the volunteer librarian returned $2.00 of her monthly $10.00 stipend, and members often made loans to the treasury to jump-start a new venture.

Almost a primer on small-town fund raising, *Bringing Books to the Ozarks* tracks the ways Branson's women rolled up their sleeves and went to work. They plucked and cleaned chickens. They cooked jitney dinners, selling meat, vegetable, and dessert portions for a nickel. They hawked magazine subscriptions door to door, served silver teas, planned fashion shows, bake sales, and turkey raffles. They sold advertising for community calendars and compiled cookbooks. They organized "This is Your Life" programs and canasta parties. They distributed bicentennial commemorative necklaces. They collected S & H green stamps and held rummage sales.

"Every year we sell packages of Georgia pecans," said Van Buskirk. "We've even sold chances on Beanie Babies."

By far, the biggest contributor to the current $67,000 budget is the library's thrift shop. Occupying half the library's ground floor, The Second Edition, supplies a third of the library's funding and requires steadfast volunteer participation to sort, price, and sell its wares.

Located in the center of Branson, the Taneyhills Community Library is a vital part of the community. Children start in the reading room downstairs, grow into the juvenile library, and then proceed upstairs to the stacks of adult fiction and non-fiction, magazine, video, audio, and computer sections. Each area requires volunteers.

"We have many members who can't get through a day without going to the library for meetings or getting something copied or repairing books or volunteering. The library is really a part of their life," said Van Buskirk.

Bringing Books to the Ozarks is about Branson as much as its books. It affirms a community spirit, which supported the Library Club's efforts. Construction, surveyors, and carpenters volunteered time and materials for building projects. School children saved small change in coffee cans. The town's official Santa Claus donated his pay, and entertainers played benefit performances. The book also documents Branson's semi-professional baseball team, torchlight tours through Marvel Cave, the effects of a new dam, a couple of wars, and the burst of neon on the town and its bookshelves. "Changing times are very evident throughout the book," said Van Buskirk.

The Library Club's monthly meetings have evolved from studying butterflies and hearing lectures on crossbreeding flowers to appearances by Tony Orlando or Barbara Fairchild. But the Club's intent, through three generations of Branson book lovers, remains the same. "A lot of people come in to enjoy the programs," said Van Buskirk. "But they understand we must have thirty to forty volunteers for the library and seventy-five volunteers for this thrift shop, every week, every day." They'd better know the drill by now. Roll up your sleeves; get to work.

Bringing Books to the Ozarks is available at the Taneyhills Community Library, (Fourth and Pacific Streets), at Barnes and Nobles Bookstores, and at the Mountaineer Book Shop in both Kirbyville and Engler Block on west Highway 76. Proceeds go to the library.

Making the Case for Knife Collecting
Shepherd Hills Cutlery

"**D**ear Sir: This knife once belonged to my dad. He passed away. He was carrying his knife when he passed away. What will it take to fix it?"

So wrote Rudy Tate to Rod Reid at Shepherd Hills Cutlery. The card's block printing, still shaky with grief, is mute tribute to the simple pocketknife and why it is cherished.

"Pocketknives have a mystic about them," said Reid. "They become a part of a person. People become attached to their knives. They carry them in their pockets all the time. In

Rod Reid of Shepherd Hills Cutlery, shows Nick Signorile and his sons, Tommy and Joe, the one-of-a-kind fifteen-blade Case knife which is displayed at Lebanon's Shepherd Hills Cutlery.

the old days, men sat and whittled and talked. Even today when I'm visiting with someone, I'll pull mine out of my pocket and just rub on it," said Reid. Because his stores, as Case outlets, advertise in *Blade Magazine,* he received Rudy's request in the mail. Rudy can't get his dad back, but his father's knife will be repaired and returned.

"What he's done is broken the tip," said Reid. "If it were an expensive knife, we'd replace the blade, but then it wouldn't be Dad's pocketknife any more. We'll make the blade a little bit shorter."

Though other companies also make pocketknives, Reid compares Case's position in the world of knives to Harley Davidson's in the motorcycle world. "These knives are more than just a product. They're not just something to open up a box. They have a history behind them. That's something people can be proud of," said Reid.

The Case knife has been around since 1899. According to Reid, it is the handle and the amount of hand production involved in the manufacturing process that makes it unique.

"Case uses a natural handle material," Reid said. "A stag knife is made from genuine antler, and a bone knife uses cattle shin bone." The antlers are imported India sandbar. Bone is harvested from five-year-old South American steers. Because U.S. feed lots butcher their animals at eighteen months, their bones don't accept color or wear as well as the more mature animal bones.

After the jigging pattern has been etched into the handle, it is dyed in a "commercial pressure cooker." Twenty-one knife components are then assembled by hand and sent to the grinding wheel for finishing. The sharp ends and edges of the knife are ground smooth and then buffed to showcase the bone or stag's natural color. Though now functional, the knife must be hafted to be saleable. Simply put, rounding the handle part's edges is a wardrobe necessity. "It'd wear a hole in your pocket otherwise," Reid said.

Though initially featuring walnut products when Reid's mother, Ida, opened Shepherd Hills in 1972, the Lebanon-based company has increasingly widened its marketing focus. Chicago Cutlery, with its walnut-handled utensils, first proposed an alliance. When Reid's Branson store manager reported frequent tourist requests for pocketknives, they approached the Case company to satisfy the demand.

As a major Case outlet since 1991, the Reid organization not only develops new ways to market the Case knife within their seven stores, it looks for new ways to attract a second generation knife collector.

Current interest in knife collecting is relatively new, emerging again after the diminishing fervor of baseball card collections. As people's interests waned of cardboard heroes, knives flashed forward, phenomena not lost on the Reid family. However, collecting old knives requires deep-pocket finances.

"People who want to collect the Case history but can't afford a five hundred dollar antique knife can buy one of these," said Reid of the several new knives his family created with Case. "We looked at why people wanted to collect those old knives. We didn't copy them, but took the desirable traits and built new knives with those features."

The most prized of all antique Case knives is the Sowbelly. Resembling a pig's swayed underside, the Sowbelly was first made in the early 1890s and was manufactured for only five years. Besides shape, the unique Sowbelly had five blades—three opening from one end, two from the other. Today an antique sowbelly would be valued between two and four thousand dollars.

Their 1995 limited edition series, proposed by Rod's brother Randy, replicated the sowbelly multiblade feature. Officially labeled "The Beast," it is a Trapper shape with a clip, razor, sheep's foot, spay, and spear blade, all opening on one end. Manufactured in seven colors and materials, each sold for about fifty dollars. Case made only one thousand of each style. Once sold from a Shepherd Hills facility in Branson, Lebanon, Osage Beach, Nashville, Eddyville (Kentucky), Huntley (Illinois), Gretna (Nevada), they've immediately become collector items. In two years, their price quadrupled. "It's probably the most popular Case knife collectible in the last twenty-five years," said Reid. "In fact, one woman at a knife show taped a sign on her back saying, "If you have a red-bone Trapper, I'll buy it."

Their second series showcased the Case's traditional tang stamp. Instead of putting the tang markings where the blade is attached to the handle, the series positions the tang stamp on a shield on the handle. The twelve variations on the tang theme also came in varying handle materials and colors.

The next series the Reid brothers and Case created was the Jaguar. Based on the old Case Cheetah, their new Jaguar featured a blade guard, which automatically locks when the six-inch blade is positioned. The difference between the new red-bone Jaguar and the antique was, again, price.

"Antique collecting can be an extremely expensive hobby. You can easily pay a thousand dollars for a knife. By collecting the new limited editions, you can get on the ground floor," said Reid. "If they go up in price, that's great.

If they don't, you have a darned good pocketknife."

Like all hobbies, knife collecting has its special vocabulary and specialization. Randy Reid collects 1920s Lady Legs knives; Rod collects letter openers. His teenage son, Ryan has the entire Beast series. "I let his be the family collection," Rod explained.

Acquiring knives can narrow into colors (red, green, mother of pearl, midnight blue) materials (bone or stag), and shapes (trappers, peanuts, or canoes).

Knife collecting is such a young specialty, and some of its founding fathers are still alive and often appear at knife shows or swap meets. Ed "Shine" Jessup, a Case representative in Tennessee, long ago encouraged customers to keep knives made from synthetic "gumfuddy" during World War II for future possible collectibles. "One of the fun things in pocketknife collecting," said Reid, "is these people are still around."

Gatherings of collectors, catalogs, clubs, and newsletters are all part of the paraphernalia. Case even produces special knives exclusively for both their adult collector's clubs and another for their junior collector group.

Grandma may have had her purse stuffed with mint candy and a crocheted handkerchief, but Grandpa carried a pocketknife. He pulled it out from deep in his overalls to clean his fingernails, cut a bull, or peel fruit. The Reids of Shepherd Hills Cutlery hope the pocketknife continues as a wardrobe accessory: to open a box, repair computer wire, or simply to collect and admire. They're doing their part to make it a Case knife.

The
Lights of
Ozark
And
Douglas
Counties

Ozark Soul

Perspective by Distance

I used to be afraid for the Ozarks. I was scared that with so much neon turned on the Plateau, it would flatten out like a shadow at high noon. I dreaded the new stores, billboards, motels, and outlet malls that popped up for

August's raspy winds pushed me down the slopes. Dodging buck-brush and spindly grass, I sought the sound of water running. (Photo by Gerald W. Dupy)

tourists. I was afraid the lines of cars and bus caravans would hit and run this region that I loved. I worried that all the concrete, plywood, insulation, and paint would simply overwhelm the Plateau, and it would die a death by suffocation.

Silly me.

One summer afternoon I took to the road, starting down the interstate to hunt the old mills of Ozark and Douglas counties. Just beyond the traffic jams and neon lights, I saw the country again and smiled as my eyes sought relics of the past: Dawt, Hodgson, Zanoni, Rockbridge, and Topaz mills. I was alone. There were no golden arches standing along the highway. No blinking signs that lit the way. No service stations. No video stores. No traffic. Just me and trees and wild flowers.

As the road narrowed to ribbons, the speed limit slowed by fives. I left asphalt for blacktop, blacktop for gravel, gravel for dirt. Ruts dug into the trail like troughs between waves. The car, my metal boat, rocked and jostled over them. Oak and hickory forests rose on either side of the faint path. The trees, webbed with underbrush, prevented my seeing the lodging or the mill or even a parking lot where I would stop until I was upon it.

Outside the car, the August heat assaulted me. The wind clacked through leaves drying on limbs. Its raspy hands pushed me down the slopes. Dodging around buckbrush and sprigs of spindly kneehigh grass, I sought the sound of water running. No ticket takers in matching cap and shirt uniforms directed where I should go. By instinct, I sought the mills. Climbing through bridge railings, I slipped down the banks, picked my way over rocks, halved both wet and dry. Beneath the overhang of dirt and roots, I walked deeper and deeper into the landscape toward the wading pool.

As I listened to the children's laughter, I balanced my feet on smoothworn rocks. It was then I stopped worrying about the Ozarks. I should have realized the Plateau is an entity bigger than anything or anyone flitting across it long before I got lost in its leaves and water murmuring.

This lesson grew at the edge of our hay field. Raised on the Illinois flat land and living in urban areas, I had no idea of the Plateau when we moved here. I had no idea what just keeping the wood stove stoked in winter would require. I learned quickly. After seeing the woodpile disappear in the cold, I thought we would soon chop all the wood on our little farm. I often wondered what we would do for heat after the trees were all gone.

Silly me.

The next spring, we wandered back where we had worked so hard. Sprouts stretched skyward from the base of the stumps and, like splayed fingers, gathered energy from the sun. The Plateau, quietly and simply, reasserted itself over what we had done.

Inside the backyard fence, near our tenacious bittersweet vine, the lesson of the Plateau lay dormant where we planted garden. That same corner had, for four decades, produced the family's vegetables before we came. Despite the tilling and hoeing and mulching and composting and raking and sifting and chopping of the soil that had gone before us, we found rocks in that plot of land. Every spring we'd push our knees deep into the cold, wet dirt to pick them up. Though we plunked them into coffee cans to carry off, the next year, without fail, this stone money of the realm appeared again. Scattered like sovereign coins over its domain, it bore the likeness of the power in charge, the Ozark Plateau.

I am less fearful now than before—less scared for the survival of the region. This is not to say the Plateau should be treated casually. The conservation of its 60,000 square miles should be a conscious effort on all our parts That, as part of our homage to it, is its due.

Still, the Ozark Plateau shook off the waters of a mighty sea. It existed before history began. It will endure. It always has. It always will. We know this. All we have to do is stand still. And look. And listen.

Down by the Riverside
Historic Mills

Dawt Mill hosts camping, float trips, and swimming on the North Fork of the White River.

A cross the hills, roads weave through fili- grees of Queen Anne's lace and blackeyed Susan wilting in the sun. While cedars menace from the forest edge, highways lose their median, and the miles between towns diminish to increments of twos or threes. Escape the crush of concrete and summer heat. Listen as sounds soften to the ruffling of brittle leaves and washing of water over smoothworn rocks. Look for tin roofs breaking through the trees— their rusted brown or silvery glint point the way.

The historic mills of Ozark and Douglas counties guard the North Fork of the White River. In an afternoon's drive from Branson, east on Missouri Highways 160 and 76, the needs of two centuries converge.

On this journey, take a picnic. There's no fast food down-stream. Take your swimming suit and a pair of wading shoes. Take your camera. Take your fishing reel or camping gear. Take, if you please, an overnight bag. Dawt, Hodgson, Zanoni, Rockbridge, and Topaz Mills each offer something different in renewal and recreation.

The Ozark mills, once dotting the waterways, grew out of necessity. Farmers, isolated in the blackjack and white oaks, needed grain ground for food. They needed equipment repaired and supplies. They needed conversation. They found material wants inside the general store, the blacksmith shop, and post office. They found community in the circle of people who waited a turn at the millstones. While corn was ground to meal and wheat to flour, children swam in the river, men competed in turkey shoots, and women cooked and chattered. It mattered little if the miller harnessed the river or a spring, whether buhrs rolled because of wheel or turbine, whether the wheels were "overshot" or "undershot."

DAWT MILL

"It was just like going to Wal-Mart," laughed Barbara Henegar, owner of Dawt Mill. "People lived out on the farm. They gathered up their corn to get processed. They had to go to the general store to get dry goods, material, and groceries. It was the social point of the community."

If any spot exemplifies the whitewater recreation that once churned at the river, it is Dawt Mill. Located twelve miles east of Gainesville on County Road PP, its three-story structure swirls with activity. Up the weatherbeaten steps, past the water moccasin skins and flour bag pictures, tourists sign in for camping, canoeing, or tube floats. Craft shelves crammed with stuffed bunnies, hats, teeshirts, and ceramic chickens lure the souvenir hunter closer in. A snack bar, bakery, and ice cream sandwiches beckon the hungry floater.

Acommodations from two-man tents to air-conditioned RVs hover in the yard. From Texas or Tennessee, campers string out the clothesline for weekend family reunions. About six hundred campsites, hidden up the hill, are available. For the less adventuresome, Dawt's original general store sleeps twenty-six. Sunbathing on the dam couldn't be better. The area is designated as a Trophy Trout Stream for its excellent rainbow and brown trout.

The present mill, built by Alva Hodgson (of Hodgson Mill fame) in 1900, was run by the water Hodgson diverted with an ingenious dam. Dawt claims continual operation since. Half-hidden behind the ice freezer, jellies, and crocheted kitchen towels, the machinery is flour dusty.

"We're the only ones to still grind like a gristmill," said Dolores Ethington, store manager.

HODGSON (AID-HODGSON) MILL

Hodgson Mill is the most famous of Missouri mills. Located twelve miles northeast of Gainesville on Highway 181, it has been featured in *National Geographic*, as well as countless tourists' snapshots. Hodgson Mill backdrops a five-foot waterfall and a millpond. The setting is a postcard for the making.

Though erected in 1861, it was bought and expanded to its present state in 1897 by Iva Hodgson. Joe Aid and Charles Wood purchased it in 1936.

"The mill was built to run a minimum of four operations at one time," said Ed Owens, caretaker. "Connected with shafts and belts, the mill powered a saw mill, a planer, a cotton gin, and the gristmill." In the 1960s, Ben Harrington installed a grinding business in the mill. When its popularity outgrew the facility, the operation moved to Gainesville. Because he copyrighted the name of the Hodgson Mill for his flour, the mill today

Lacking the massive turbines that once worked the grinding wheel, the Hodgson Mill stands quiet as a picture postcard in the making.

receives neither profit nor royalty.

"Camping pays our expenses," said Owens, referring to the twenty-five electrical and water hookups and numerous primitive sites which surround the mill. Structurally sound, the mill's timbers need little maintenance. Twenty-five million gallons of spring water powered it until the steel turbines were removed for repair.

Not much goes on in the gift store inside the mill. The real activity is a stone's throw from the mill's water wheel. The laughter echoes across a century. Modern-day teens spend the afternoon cannon-balling into Bryant Creek and splashing cars that cross the bridge. Adults, seated on lawn chairs in the water, visit while children squeal in the sand and sun.

ZANONI MILL

"My grandparents bought this place in 1905 and ran the mill, store, and post office," said David Morrison, the only present-day owner with any ties to the mill's origi-

nators. "When he died in 1969, the place was sold to a St. Louis developer. I bought it in 1976."

Smallest of the mills, the Zanoni Mill has the only work-able "overshot" water wheel, designed so spring water turns the pad-dles by pouring over them. The Mill, the Morrison General Store,

Water still turns the overshot construction of Zanoni Mill. (Photo courtesy of Bittersweet, Inc.)

and Granny Home sit like green-and-white toys around the modern Morrison home.

Located six miles north of Gainesville on Highway 181, the Morrison home spreads ten-thousand square feet across the back of a three-acre lake. The south wing, with natural rock fireplace and cathedral ceiling, encloses an eighteen by thirty-six heated pool and hot tub. A front porch swing hangs on the balcony. The basement has pool and ping pong tables.

The colonial mansion is a bed and breakfast inn. Up the spiraled staircase and past the floor-to-ceiling mirrors are four guest bedrooms. Plush carpet, cross-stitched pillows, embroidered curtains, stuffed toys, and family pictures suggest a welcome better suited to long-absent relatives than paying guests. The aroma of hot biscuits, sizzling bacon, and ham omelet coax the hungry downstairs. Served under the dining room's crystal chandelier, the table is graced with fresh-picked blueberries and Mary Morrison's smiling face.

Most guests arrive at the circular drive from St. Louis, Kansas City, Memphis, or Tulsa. Some seek trout fishing. Others arrive to celebrate anniversaries, honeymoons, or family reunions. Besides their normal April-October season, the Morrisons' book Valentine's Day and New Year's Eve.

ROCK BRIDGE MILL

Rockbridge Mill completes the loop of historic mills. It requires a turn on County Road N, and a fifteen mile drive north on Highway 181. Now a mere shell, the mill provides scenery to the resort's star attraction—fish to catch, fish to watch being

Rockbridge Mill, owned by the Amyx family, marks where rainbow trout line up like dominos at the dam nearby.

caught, and fish to eat.

Rainbow Trout Ranch and Rockbridge Gun Club are situated on Morris Creek as it runs through the Amyx family's eighteen-hundred acre property. The twenty-nine cabins, nine beds in the "White House" or three beds in the "New House" require reservations.

"What brings people here is the peace and quiet," said owner Ray Amyx. "We have excellent food, no hassle, no phones, no television, no alarm clocks, no radio."

Things have changed little over time. The mill towers above the dam and the two-pound rainbow trout line up like dominoes in spring-fed waters. No state license is required nor official limit enforced. Customers pay two dollars and fifty cents for a permit and three dollars a pound for the fish they catch.

The less adept with rod and reel can still enjoy the best fish around, baked, broiled, panfried, filleted, or almondined at the Rainbow Trout Farm Restaurant. Only reservations guarantee a table.

The facility's sporting clay range is located away from the mill's tranquil setting. Guns and shells are available for practice.

TOPAZ MILL

Topaz Mill is the crown jewel in this circle of mills. Marigolds, zinnias, and fresh redwood paint belie the respect owner Joe O'Neal gives to its past. Located fourteen miles southwest of Cabool, it requires a five-mile descent off Missouri Highway 76, either on County roads E or EE. While road maintenance ends and gravel roads disintegrate into dirt, the view around the corner, over the slab bridge, and past the spring is worth the trip. "I don't mind if people come to see it," said

O'Neal. "I figure if they came this far, they must be pretty interested."

Each October, Topaz Mill is centerpiece for community activities. The rural firefighter's annual fund raiser brings five hundred visitors to the quiet setting.

Years ago, a general store, a blacksmith shop, cannery, barber shop, and a post office grouped together, all a respectful distance from the mill. These buildings stand today.

In fact, not much disturbs the tranquility until the third week in October when (since 1986) the Topaz Mill has hosted the rural firefighters' fund raiser. Five hundred people park their cars in the grass for the baked potato, grilled pork, and barbecued chicken that's prepared in the shade of the mill.

"We serve until people quit eating or we run out of food," O'Neal said. "And we've never run out of food."

Edged in moss and poxed by the touch of a million water bugs, the spring daily sends ten million gallons of water into the North Fork of the White River. Only a plywood board prevents it from flowing down the trace to the mill's turbines. Though the machinery is still intact, it hasn't been used in sixty years. A few hundred yards down the gravel road, people still congregate at "the swimming hole" on a hot afternoon.

EDWARDS MILL

Back at Branson, at the College of the Ozarks, Edwards Mill

grinds sixteen thousand pounds of corn and a thousand pounds of wheat a month. "We still stone grind the old fashioned way," said Jim Davis, supervisor of the mill. "Nothing is different except a dust collector. We even still use the old sewing machines and paper bags to sew it up."

The mill machinery, shining and spotless, can be run either by electricity or water-powered by the fourteen-foot overshot water wheel. Opened in 1972, Edwards Mill is a really a replica, constructed of discarded parts rescued from the other mills. The hundred-year-old iron hubs were salvaged from Jackson Mill near Ava. The timbers, now over two hundred years old, were previously used in the Globe Mill, City Mill, and Cowgill and Hill Mill near Carthage.

The forty-eight-inch and thirty-eight-inch buhrs grind grain purchased from a northern Missouri farm. "We know our flour is pure," said Davis. "We make it the old fashioned way—none of this self-rising stuff."

Herbert and Alice Edwards erected the mill as a workstation at the college. During fall and winter semesters, twenty-five students operate the mill. Only fifteen students work eight-hour shifts in summer's slack time. Though grinding is done as needed, Davis said the mill usually grinds Tuesday and Thursday mornings. Open Monday through Saturday, the mill also has a weaving studio upstairs.

Although the historic mills are privately owned, there is talk of placing them on the National Register of Historic Places. Perhaps they should be. The mills are Missouri treasures. Once outposts of civilization, they now offer sanctuary from it, cooling weary minds and aching spirits in the waters of the past.

Heavenly Fruitcake

Assumption Abbey Bakers

"People say, 'Get even, send fruit-cake,'" joked Brother Dominic, as he decorated the holiday dessert his Abbey brothers make. "But they haven't tasted ours."

The fruitcake's reputation tradition-

Assumption Abbey has housed the fifteen members of the Cisterian Order since 1950.

ally stems from a density that could devastate tall buildings and candy that cements the teeth. On the other hand, the Assumption Abbey fruitcake is moist, chewy with nuts, sub-tly flavored with nutmeg, cinnamon, citron, and laced with holiday spirit.

From February through November, the fifteen Trappist monks who live high in the Ozark mountains divide their day between spiritual meditation and baking the fruitcakes which support them. "We're an Abbey that happens to be a bakery," said Father Theodore, the Abbey's business manager, "not a bakery that is an Abbey."

Rising at 3:30 a.m., the men calmly attend their baking duties between Vigils, Lauds, Terce, and Mass. Their daily Eternal quota: seven services of prayer. Their daily production quota: one hundred twenty-five two-pound fruitcakes. Eight hours after marinating, mixing, measuring, baking, cooling, decorating, flavoring, and packaging their wares, Brothers Theodore, Bernard, and James leave a clean kitchen for midday chapel.

Since 1950, the Cisterian Order has maintained a monastery high among the Ozark ridges, ninety minutes east from Branson or two hundred miles southwest of St. Louis. Past Ava, and the smaller villages of Rome and Squires, Assumption Abbey is hard to find. The route lines fade on the map from red to black to gray. Even the numbers diminish as the road ascends to the crest of the mountain. From Branson, take Missouri 76 east to Missouri 5 to County Road N to Country Road 00. Beyond hairpin turns and above foliage wreathing the horizon, the men live quietly on thirty-four hundred acres given to them by Chicago newspaperman, Joseph Pierson. Part of him still remains at the Abbey.

"Originally a St. Louis cooperage bought small farms and took all the white oak for whiskey barrels," explained Father Theodore. "It sold out to Mr. Pierson, who was living in Tulsa. His wife died after we had been here awhile. A couple of years later, he remarried. When he died, he was cremated. Half of him is buried here; the second half is buried in Tulsa with his first wife. When his second wife died, she was buried here with him. So the circle is complete, and we have fourteen and a half people in our cemetery."

With the aroma of mace and Puerto Rican rum drifting through the air, the brother's litany echoes *Brother Dominic places the four citrons and four pecans on the Abbey's heavenly fruitcakes.* against the stained glass and polished marble floors of their spartan chapel. Their unison chants curl around the morning. Part of their purpose, beyond the kitchen door, is to provide a quiet place for spiritual retreat. Annually, about six hundred visitors use the nine guestrooms for rest and renewal.

Supporting the Abbey hasn't been easy. Though unafraid of demanding work, the men discovered the hills' scant topsoil could not support the traditional farming ventures their order employs in Iowa. Cattle, grapes, and apples did not flourish near the pine tree line. For two decades, they tried manufacturing concrete blocks until declining sales and the physical demands on the aging men forced them to look for other means of support.

"We explored everything from growing mushrooms to fishponds to wooden palletes. Nothing fit our community," said Father Theodore.

They consulted other Trappist monasteries. Three of the seventeen communities bake fruitcakes; others make jams, jellies, and fudge.

"When television newscasters Lehrner and McNeil did a piece on us, they had fun with that one," said Father Theodore. "They said when we switched from making concrete to fruitcakes, we just changed the product but kept using the same equipment."

Of course, they didn't. The Assumption Abbey brothers experimented with recipes, local and family favorites, trying to find one that would move the fruitcake's reputation from doorstop to delicacy. Then Mrs. Everett Salmon, who had rested her strained voice in the Abbey's peaceful setting, steered them toward St. Louis chef Jean-Pierre Auge and eight English high-tea recipes. The brothers eventually chose Auge's personal favorite, the one once served to the Duke and Duchess of Windsor.

The Abbey's fruitcake really is a fruit cake, comprised of seventy percent pineapple, cherries, white currants, walnuts, and both golden and dark raisins. The mixture marinates three days in burgundy before it is mixed with flour-egg-milk batter. Too thick for machinery, the mixture must be stirred by hand.

While the brothers now courteously decline to share their recipe, Father Theodore explained, "It's no secret. Several English women say it's just like the one their mothers baked. One lady, Sadie from Mississippi, sent us a sample of hers. It was almost identical. So find Sadie, and you've got it."

The Kentucky monastery, whose automated assembly produces forty thousand cakes, offered advice about mechanics. "A St. Louis bakery donated used pans and racks. The brothers enlarged the recipe's serving size from six to one hundred twenty.

"Auge said it was a miracle," laughed Father Theodore. "Brother Kevin, our cook, got it right the first time."

The brothers peddled their product by mouth. "Whenever I'd go to stores to take orders, I just give them a bite, and that was that," said Father Theodore. Their unassuming white tin can be found in gift, cheese, coffee shops, and specialty catalogs, like William Sonoma's. Their first six thousand sold out. Eight years later, having quadrupled their numbers, the monks are hard pressed to fill orders that come in by phone, fax, CompuServe, or Prodigy.

"I guess the personal touch is part of the secret," said Father Theodore. The small kitchen and closet-sized work rooms have no space for anything so commercialized as conveyer-belt clatter. Besides, a much bigger business would steal too much of the Order's serenity. "We want to do the work ourselves in a home atmosphere. It's part of the rhythm of our lives."

The magic number at the Abbey is two. Dressed in their order's black and white habit, the men divide the responsibilities into pairs. Two combine the marinated fruit with the dry ingredients by hand. Brother James measures the dough into two-pound pans while Brother Anthony smoothes the tops with a tablespoon. The cakes bake two hours. After an overnight cooling, two other brothers take the cakes out of the pans. Then Brother Dominic and Brother Guerric supply the finishing touches. Using a syringe, Brother Dominic injects one ounce of Puerto Rican gold rum, eight jabs to each cake. Later he carefully decorates the top, patterning two cherries, two citrons, and two pairs of pecans. Brother Guerric brushes the cake with corn syrup to seal in moisture. The next day he fuses the cellophane wrappers in place with a household plate warmer two cakes at a time. Sealed tight, the cakes are placed in tins for distribution.

"A man who got one of our fruitcakes as a gift called us up. He found it in a closet and didn't know how long it had been there," recalled Father Theodore. "He wanted to know if it was still safe to eat. I got one I had been saving since 1992, and we opened them together. When I pulled off the wrapper, the aroma just filled the room. It was wonderful. And yes, it was safe to eat."

Though their sellout success could expand into a factory enterprise, the Trappists of Assumption Abbey will not yield to the temptation—any more than they would overlook the "Thou Shalt Not Steal" warning on their Friar Tuck cookie jar. The fifteen-member work force and their four-hour time slots remain the same.

"We went to one hundred twenty-five a day by adding an extra cake to five trays," admitted Father Theodore. "That way we can still process in the same time.

The Trappist brothers bake their two pound fruitcakes from February to November.

But twenty-three thousand is about our limit."

Besides, working in their forty-year-old kitchen is a squeeze. They stand on stools and juggle equipment about the room. Without air conditioning, baking in Missouri's summer is a trial by fire.

Considering a new facility, they weighed the advantages of automating and found it lacking. "After we finished with the machine, we'd have to break it down," said Father Theodore. "It won't save much time if we have to take it apart to clean it. Besides, we won't do anything that changes the recipe. What we hear most often is: 'I don't like fruitcake, but I like yours.'"

The monks take pleasure in the fruitcakes they've sent to every state as well as in England, France, Germany, Canada, and Finland. Their conversation is full of playful puns about eating their mistakes and savoring the marinating fruit's distinctive aroma. Their good humor extends to collecting Far Side cartoons and keeping a folder of Broom Hilda and Geeta fruitcake jokes.

"I have a card that reads 'Just say no to fruitcakes,'" said Father Theodore.

If fruitcake has been the curse of Christmas, the Assumption Abbey bakes a blessing. Made by hand, created with care, their holiday dessert should be brightly wrapped and set under the tree—just like all the other good things of the season.

Ozarker Writes "Little House" Books
Laura Ingalls Wilder

A two-story, white frame farmhouse sits on a gentle hill just outside Mansfield, Missouri. Above the road, like a setting hen on the nest, the structure looks settled and comfortable. Circled by oak trees and lush greenery, the porch and stone chimney needs only a mistress shaking her dust rag outside the door or carrying a water bucket to the chickens.

Such a woman once resided in this house. To the town, she was the wife of farmer A.J. Wilder. To the world, she was

Laura Ingalls Wilder, distinguished author. To children everywhere, she was "Half Pint," pioneer heroine of the "Little House" books.

Impressions to the contrary, Laura Ingalls Wilder did

Laura and Almanzo Wilder lived nearly sixty years in their small farmhouse outside Mansfield, Missouri.

not always live at Walnut Grove, Minnesota. Nor was she a writer of messianic ambitions. She lived sixty-three of her ninety years in Mansfield, forty miles east of Springfield. After hop scotching across Wisconsin, Minnesota, the Dakotas, and Kansas as a child, she became an adopted Ozarker whose roots took hold of the rocky terrain and never let go. She lived quietly and busily as a wife and mother. Her writing career developed and flourished incidentally in her already full life.

The A.J. Wilders arrived in Mansfield in 1894, seeking a milder climate and better luck than they found in De Smet, South Dakota. Their homesteading efforts on the High Plains had been thwarted by hailstorms, drought, fire, sickness, and debt. Almanzo's health was permanently bruised by diphtheria and a stroke. Their infant son died there.

Intrigued by a railroad pamphlet's descriptions, they loaded a covered wagon with their belongings and seven-year-old daughter, Rose, and headed to the "Land of the Big Apple"—Missouri. After forty-five days and six hundred fifty miles, they reached the Show-Me State. Laura liked what she saw:

> Well, we are in the Ozarks at last, just the beginning of them, and they are beautiful. We passed along the front of some hills and could look up their sides. The trees and rocks are lovely. Manly said we could almost live on the looks of them.

Six days later, the Wilders passed through Springfield, a booming town of 21,850. Laura noted:

> It is a thriving city with fine houses and four busi-

ness blocks stand around a town square. The stores are
well stocked and busy. Manly hitched the horses and
we bought shoes for Rose and myself, a calico dress for
me and a new hat for Manly. It did not take much time
and we drove right along through the city. It is the
nicest city we have seen yet. It is simply grand.

Once in Mansfield, "the Gem City of the Ozarks," Almanzo found a forty-acre farm site with a one-room log cabin, a spring, four cleared acres, and four hundred apple trees, waiting to be planted. On Rocky Ridge Farm, their fortunes changed. The land, though wild and tangled, responded to the Wilders' hard work. With Laura at the other end of the crosscut saw, Almanzo cleared timber, sowed grass, and planted an orchard. Firewood that sold for seventy cents a wagon load and eggs helped buy groceries. After selling their first crop of potatoes, the Wilders bought a cow and a pig. Laura's homemaking duties stretched to include straining milk, making butter, and baking bread.

She wrote wryly: *"No one seems to want to work like a farmer except the farmer's wife."* Ironically, it was Laura's flock of leghorns that led her to a more literary activity. Since her chickens were reputed to be among the best in the area, she frequently was asked to explain her success. Once, when she couldn't leave the farm, her speech was read at the farm meeting. The *Missouri Ruralist's* editor heard it and asked her to join his staff. Although she protested at first with, "I've never graduated from anything and only attended high school two years," she took the job. Her column, "As a Farm Woman Thinks" by Mrs. A.J. Wilder, ran from 1911 to 1924. Later, she became poultry editor for the *St. Louis Star* and contributed to *State Farmer, St. Louis Globe Democrat, McCall's, Country Gentlemen,* and *St. Nicholas.*

In the meantime, she remained involved with the Methodist Episcopal Church (South), Eastern Star, and the Athenian club, a cultural organization working toward bringing Mansfield a library.

In 1931, another direction emerged for Laura Ingalls Wilder, the writer. After thirty-five years of farming, the Wilders decided to slow down. Almanzo sold off portions of their now two-hundred acre farm. Laura resigned her writing positions. But a comment by her daughter, Rose, launched Laura's new career.

Irene Lichty LeCount, once curator of the Laura Ingalls Wilder-Rose Wilder Lane Museum said: "She (Laura) told me she had a letter from Rose asking her to write down the stories she had told her as a little girl. She wrote down some and sent them to Rose. Rose sent them on. Laura was encouraged by a note from the *Harper* editor who wrote: *This is good, but put some meat on it.*"

At sixty-five, Mrs. A.J. Wilder became Laura Ingalls Wilder, book author. On a 50-50 school tablet bought from a Springfield grocery store she wrote *Little House in the Big Woods,* detailing the experiences of Laura and Mary Ingalls in Wisconsin. "That book was a labor of love and is really a memorial to my father," Laura Ingalls Wilder later said. "I did not expect much from the book, but hoped that a few children might enjoy the stories I had loved."

Public clamor about the Ingalls family pressed Laura Ingalls Wilder to write more. In 1935, *Farmer Boy* chronicled Almanzo's growing up years in New York. In 1935, *Little House on the Prairie* continued the Ingalls' adventures in

Indian Territory (Kansas). Laura summarized:

> *Here, instead of woods and bears and deer as in the*
> *Big Woods or horses, cows, pigs and schools as so*
> *many years ago in* Farmer Boy *were wild Indians,*
> *wolves, prairie fires, rivers in flood and U.S. soldiers.*

While in Minnesota, the Ingalls had lived in a sod house. *On the Banks of Plum Creek* told how they endured a plague of grasshoppers and blizzards. *By the Shores of Silver Lake* (1939) followed a story recounting the time "Pa" worked for the railroad. The Ingalls moved to town in *The Long Winter* (1940), and in *Little Town on the Prairie* (1941) Laura received her teaching certificate.

Children readily accepted Laura Ingalls Wilder's broad-stroked character sketches. They understood "Pa" could be both the family's protector, fending off the wild during the day, as well as an affectionate father, calling his girls to his knee each night. "Ma" quietly expected her children to "be nice girls." The family's survival hinged on the adults' resourcefulness and perseverance.

In *These Happy Golden Years* (1943) "Half Pint" (teaching at a school twelve miles from home) is courted by Almanzo. Though continually pressed for another installment of her life, she never published another book.

A secret manuscript, found after Laura's death, was not published until daughter, Rose, died in 1968. *The First Four Years*, printed exactly as Laura wrote it in her tablet, recounts the overwhelming obstacles she and Almanzo fought homesteading in South Dakota.

"I don't think Mrs. Wilder ever intended for it to be published," said Irene Lichty LeCount. "Most readers are happy they have it, but they can tell it's not as refined as the other books."

Nevertheless, children wrote asking for more stories and sent birthday, Valentine, and Christmas greetings. In their great outpouring of affection, some wrote a casual correspondence to their friend, Laura, while others addressed, stiffly and formally, the celebrated author. Classes sent paper mache models of "Jack the Dog" and "Black Susan the Cat," as well as a covered wagon replicas, and corn husk dolls of the Ingalls' family.

Literary recognition was as immediate as public recognition. Laura's first book was runner up for the Newberry Award. She won the Harry Hartman Award of the Pacific Northwest Library Association. These Happy Golden Years garnered the New York Herald Tribune's Spring Book Festival Prize. In 1954, the Children's Library Association created the Laura Ingalls Wilder Award, which honors an author who makes a lasting contribution to children's literature. Libraries in Detroit, Michigan, Ponoma, California, and Mansfield have included Laura's name as part of the library's title.

Yet, surprisingly, Laura's writing did not dominate her life. Putting her past into books was just one more project to accomplish besides preparing breakfast, washing dishes, making beds, or walking to the mailbox. "It really was incidental to her," said LeCount. "Her home, husband, and daughter were the important things in her life. She was happy they (the books) were well received. She said, "If my books help one child, I'll be happy.' Of course, they've helped thousands."

In 1957, L.D. and Irene Lichty approached Laura about

a memorial. "I asked Mrs. Wilder about it. She didn't give any answer except to say, 'My house has gotten pretty shabby,' but I found out through Rose, her mother was really pleased," said LeCount.

The Lichtys opened the Laura Ingalls Wilder Home in May, three months after Laura's death. Though the exhibits were originally placed in the home, a separate building was later built, and both are now run by a private corporation. Open from May to October, the project accommodates about fifty thousand visitors a season. Admission and gifts sustain it.

The museum and home display three faces of this remarkable woman. There are Mrs. A. J. Wilder's pink depression glassware, handmade quilts, her modern kitchen's unusual hot and cold water faucets, and electric toaster. Furniture her husband fashioned from cypress roots and tree branches are there, too. The rooms also accommodate the famous author. Clippings of Laura Ingalls Wilder's awards and honors line the walls. The living room houses a portrait of Almanzo and Laura in a covered wagon, a gift from the art editor of Saturday Evening Post. The manuscripts which created Laura Ingalls are on display. Items from the "Little House" books—"Pa's" fiddle, Mary's organ, and Laura's first needlepoint samplers are among the row upon row of memorabilia.

Today, the museum and LeCount seem the best sources about the famous residents of Rocky Ridge Farm. The most common question asked of LeCount as she presided at the museum's front desk is "How did you like the TV program?"

It takes very little to learn her dim view of the small-screen representation of the Little House books. "There are so many things in the books they could have used," said

LeCount. "There is a scene where Indians left South Kansas. Laura watched them. There were so many papooses she asked Pa to get her one. Without too much embellishment that could have been quite dramatic—and it actually happened. Of course, the longer it was on, the further away it got. We received a letter from England saying, 'Please write me about the adopted children.' Of course," said LeCount icily, "there weren't any."

In September, Mansfield celebrates Laura Ingalls Wilder Days. Residents put on old-time dresses, participate in rail splitting, games, and beard contests. A parade with floats take a "Little House" theme.

Except for the festival, a billboard or two, and her name on the library and local cafeteria, Mansfield makes little of the bright life that once lived there. Laura Wilder would have liked it that way.

Though she would disclaim it, Laura Ingalls Wilder was a complex woman. At Rocky Ridge, she slipped in and out of her roles as easily as putting on an apron. Wife, mother, homemaker, tender of chicks, author, historian, and story teller were all hers. Though the farm wife and author died in February, 1957, Laura, the pioneer girl, lives on in the "Little House" books and in the hearts of the young who read them.

85-year-old Laura Ingalls Wilder autographs books in 1952. (Photo courtesy of Laura Ingalls Wilder Home Association.)

Outhouse Ideas

LeRoy Walls

I t all started in the outhouse. Hunched over the lingerie section of Sears and Roebuck catalog, LeRoy Walls tried to keep his twelve-year-old mind on his business and off the February wind that bothered his butt in the family's outdoor facilities. "I tell people my first goal for the bathroom was to have it inside the house," he said.

Today, LeRoy sits quite comfortably elsewhere. As Chief Executive Officer of Woodpro Cabinetry, Inc., he oversees the manufacturing of bathroom cabinetry from the red oak timber of Missouri hills. Twenty different cabinet options branch into four different price categories. The company supplies cabinetry for thirty group companies in twenty-five states. It cuts, assembles, stains, and ships six thousand pieces a month and was an eight million-dollar business in 1997.

If Ozark wood is the material of Woodpro's vanities, medicine cabinets, and linen closets, an Ozark value notched it there. Though owned by two Walls brothers, the employees relate on an extended family tree. Wives, husbands, siblings, children, work every area from marketing

The Walls family privy inspired LeRoy Walls to enter the bathroom cabinetry business. (Photo courtesy of LeRoy Walls)

to accounts payable. Production workers are considered "adopted cousins" whose stake in the company extends beyond the time clock.

The business began in 1977 when LeRoy and his brother, Keith, teamed up in Keith's custom cabinet shop. It was an opportunity for LeRoy, a St. Louis data processor and his wife, Paula, a registered nurse, to raise their children in Cabool, their hometown.

The brothers worked together for three years and then parted amiably. Keith remained in retail custom cabinetry. LeRoy concentrated on the wholesale manufacturing line of bathroom fixtures. "We liked each other too much to hassle each other," LeRoy recalled of the split. "We just had different ideas for business growth. My brother expected a two-person shop, and I expected a coordinated, expanding shop."

LeRoy moved down the street and across the tracks into an empty poultry plant. In twenty-one years, the facility has grown to seventy thousand square feet and employs a hundred people. None of it happened easy. In the beginning, LeRoy marketed the old fashioned way, with his foot to the pedal and his eyes on the street.

"I wasn't very scientific, but I worked hard at it. I showed my first cabinets in the back of my pickup. That's how we got our first major account in 1978. Later, we just drove around looking for the biggest home center type store in town."

The next sales van was a used bread truck with a hundred thousand miles on it. LeRoy carpeted and wallpapered it, and installed three sets of cabinets. "You get a buyer inside and guard the door, and you'll have a real good chance of making a sale," he said.

Today, website pages make advertising a different world. Glen, LeRoy's younger brother, now Vice President in charge of marketing, tracks buyers, their location, and volume. Customers dot the map in Ohio, Michigan, Indiana, Illinois, Florida, Minnesota, and New York. Missourians find Woodpro products in Meek's, HWI Stores, and National Stores.

Early on, Woodpro offered unusual features in bath products. It was one of the first companies to make a wood medicine cabinet and to add the simple towel bar at the bottom of the cabinet. More recently, it has included a breakfront design on both products.

Woodpro cabinetry begins as red oak boards harvested in Salem, Missouri. Every other day, ten thousand board feet are shipped to Cabool in planks, already planed, and kiln dried.

"Around here people call it black oak, but it's the red oak species," said LeRoy. "In cabinetry, ninety percent is red oak. White oak is more expensive because of the stave market."

Woodpro gets its wood from LeRoy's former high school shop teacher, Leon Seneker. "He knew Jerry was just getting started. In our conversation, he suggested maybe we had red oak lumber in common. We did, and now we work real closely with him."

The planks are ripped to proper width, sanded, and begin a circuitous route through the building to be glued or grooved, stained or varnished, assembled, and packaged. It is a process that has been carefully planned by LeRoy. "We have a lot of discipline in the way we build cabinets. We use a lot of Japanese manufacturing technology."

With no warehouse or inventory, Woodpro operates on a wood-in-cabinet-out construction policy. "We don't do all the twenty-four-inch cabinets at one time and then keep them around. Using mixed-model scheduling, the line makes twenty-four, forty-eight or eighteen inchers in whatever order they need to be put on the truck," said LeRoy.

LeRoy also solicits self-improvement ideas from his production staff. A reward, up to a dozen two dollar bills, generates one and a half times the American industry's usual number of suggestions for adjustments or safety. "We don't get fifty ideas a year. We get two thousand ideas a year."

The Walls brothers grew up on one hundred twenty acres outside Cabool. "We had a dozen cows that had names. Our fifty or so chickens were a mom-and-kids project. We butchered our pigs and sold a few," LeRoy recalled. Today he cuts a straight line from his childhood to the principle, which runs and markets his business. "Uptown cabinetry and down home service" distinguishes the company from the others who set up display booths at industry shows. Newsletters, calendars, and price lists are decorated with photos his mother took with her black box Brownie of the family haying in the field, playing in the woodpile, or visit-

LeRoy Walls, CEO of Woodpro Cabinetry, Inc., stands before the map marking destinations for his Ozark-built bathroom cabinets.

ing the general store. His short anecdotes about his dog, Walter, or the water pump, or the accident on his brother's Western Flyer remind clients of the values of loyalty, hard work, or safety program found inside Woodpro's plant. He playfully lists employee relationships: "Susie is Missy's mother. Tammy is Leona's daughter. Jack is David's son, and Bob is Kurt's father. Mary and Steve are married to twins, and Gene and Dale are brothers-in-law. Kelly and Melvin, Debbie and Larry, Jamie and Gleneta, Kurt and Lisa are married." He then explained that to Woodpro, hiring family members means hiring known integrity and work ethic.

The business is a hands-on operation for his family. Paula, his wife, works in accounting and finance. One daughter, Sarah Montgomery, is Vice President in charge of Operations and another, Lora Noll, is Director of Customer Service. During peak periods, like filling the orders for Carter Lumber's one hundred eighty stores, everyone helps the production line. "I rotate where I work so I can learn about problems and let the staff know I'm pitching in," the CEO said.

The emergence of Home Depot or Builders' Square

warehouses have had an undeniable effect on the market. While tempted to court the megabusinesses, putting the future of the company on one large account gives Leroy pause.

"The direction we've gone without the giants has been pretty successful," he said. "It's not as risky to us having a lot of smaller customers. I think we have a good product. We have good people. We have a good system, and we've taken our role with customers seriously," he said.

For a man whose success began on his backside, LeRoy Walls has come a long way from the two-holer out by the barn. The red oak forest, the family, and hard work have brought him in from the cold.

The Lights of OZARK AND NIXA

Birthing Big Babies

Dr. Ruth E. Massey, Veterinarian

W hat happens after you deliver a giraffe? Get off the ladder. What happens after you encourage an alligator's love life? Get out of the way.

Specializing in large animal reproduction keeps Dr. Ruth Massey on her toes. Her patients, whether by length or height or width, can outsize her by six feet or outweigh her by two and a half tons. And some are not grateful for her care.

Dr. Ruth E. Massey left alligators and giraffes in the South for Percharons and the region of her youth. (Photo by Bob Linder, Springfield (M.O.) News-Leader.)

Ruth's mobile practice in Christian and Greene counties includes the equine, from two-ton draft horses to standard breed to two-hundred pound miniatures, with dogs, cats, and an occasional llama thrown in. Treating African wildlife occurred during her advanced studies for Board Certification in Reproduction at the University of Florida.

"Artificial insemination, for the male alligator, was a terminal experience," she recalled. "They were making such a comeback in Florida that nuisance 'gators—ones that got in a backyard or pool—were captured by licensed 'gator hunters. In breeding season, they'd call us, then kill the 'gator. They'd harvest the meat and hide, and we'd harvest the semen. We'd then tranquilize the female with Valium, tape her mouth, and inseminate her."

The giraffe she treated couldn't deliver a mis-positioned calf. Rather than anesthetize an animal that could break its neck getting to ground level, Ruth and another vet assisted on their tip toes. "The giraffe was so tall, we stood on a fourteen-foot step ladder," said Ruth. "The calf was all turned around. The other vet worked until his arm got tired. Then I tried. We straightened the head and feet, and it came through."

Getting her veterinarian degree was several rungs up the ladder for Ruth. She's been working with animals since she split responsibilities with her brother on the family farm south of Lebanon. "We were to take turns cooking and doing chores," said Ruth. "I decided I'd rather be outside. What I loved about the horses was raising the foals."

But when Ruth, as a teenager, looked at career choices, women rarely enrolled in veterinarian school. "In 1972, there were two women in a class of sixty. The policy was to increase the class by two each year. I didn't even try because I was told–'Don't.'"

Instead, she picked up both a bachelor's and a master's degree in English. While teaching and then working for the Social Security Administration, she kept tight rein on her first love.

"In four years, the whole attitude changed," said Ruth. "By then women made up one third of the classes. We were encouraged to apply."

In 1982, she stepped up to her dream. She returned to school, completing science prerequisites in two years. In four more she obtained her DVM degree from the University of Missouri. Ruth shortly headed for a two-year residency at the University of Florida. "If it had anything to do with reproduction in any species, we saw it there," she said.

Sometimes she saw it again and again. Every week Ruth and a clinician spent all day at a large dairy farm, pregnancy testing cows in four-hundred-head batches. "That did it for me," she said. "I haven't palpated a cow in five years, and I intend to keep it that way."

After three years in a Florida practice, the pull of the Ozarks brought Ruth back to Springfield, Board Certification in hand. With three hundred others nationwide, Ruth's is the only private practice in southwest Missouri with this designation. Though she sees dogs, cats, and an occasional goat, her patients are primarily equine. "This is a horsy area because of the state's agricultural roots and its economics," said Ruth. "People have money to take care of their animals. This is also a center of fox trotters. I see a lot of quarter horses and saddle breds, too."

Foaling season spans March and June. "I'm working a ninety-hour week then, " she said. "I leave at seven a.m. and get back at ten p.m., seven days a week. I tell myself I can sleep in November and December."

Though the office in her home is cluttered with fox trotter and equine reproduction books, arm-length disposable gloves, horse statues, eqvalan paste, and sponge gauze, Ruth's real center of operations is her truck. On the road forty thousand miles a year, she carries ultrasound, x-ray, computer, and printer with her.

Working with large animals is a gender equalizer. "On a pound-for-pound basis, no woman or man is going to out muscle an eleven-hundred-pound animal," said Ruth. "I tell my clients, 'That's why God made tranquilizers.'"

Still, Ruth's respect for her patients translates into a soft-spoken compassion. "You have to understand how a horse thinks and read its body language," said Ruth. "If you respond, most of the time it's amazing what these animals will let us do to them. I wouldn't tolerate what I do to them."

Much of equine obstetrics requires a shoulder-length reach into the animal's rectum, either to feel with the hand or to guide the ultrasound probe toward the uterus. Communicating with the animal requires reading the eyes, ears, and tail. To reach a Percheron's, Ruth requires a concrete block or a position uphill of the mare. Under her careful touch, the mammoth draft horse often nonchalantly eats grain.

"What with ultrasound and rectal palpations, I'm behind a horse a thousand times in a year. Two thirds of the time, there is very little restraint on it, and I've got kicked just one time."

No wonder she gave up alligators.

Singing the Sad Songs
Judy Domeny

"I'm the Queen of Death and Dying," admitted Judy Domeny. She's got a point. Hangings, poisonings, kidnapping, orphans, star-struck lovers, widowed mothers, and wounded soldiers drape the folk singer's repertoire in black. Unfortunately, her songs are historically correct.

"Most are sad because they were reflections of people's lives," said Judy. "Death came at an earlier age. Children died young, or mothers died in childbirth."

For twenty-six of her thirty-eight years, the Rogersville resident has been wrapping her clear, vibrant voice around the melancholy. A familiar figure on the

During the week, she's Mrs. Bowen, elementary school art teacher. On weekends, she's folk singer, Judy Domeny, "The Queen of Death and Dying."

festival-and-fair circuit, she's inventoried about two hundred songs for her six concert topics. Without fancy costuming or amplification, Domeny and guitar have toured Kansas, Oklahoma, Arkansas, Iowa, Kentucky, and Illinois. She's sung from Stockton's Walnut Festival to Booneville's Big Muddy Folk Festival to Mansfield's Laura Ingalls Wilder Days. She's a perennial performer at Silver Dollar City and has two recordings, "Calling Me Back" and "Yesterday's News." "No part of the state is safe," she said.

Folk singing is Judy's lifetime passion, threading between education degrees at Drury College and Southwest Missouri State University, teaching, working as an auctioneer, playing farmer, and song writing. Domeny began traveling her musical trail of tears at twelve after finding a booklet on a family outing. "I was taking guitar lessons and singing country songs. Our family visited the Laura Ingalls Wilder Museum. I found some folk songs I thought I could play. My dad showed me "Letter Edged in Black" and said my grandma had taught it to him. I thought it would be nice to learn something they both knew."

The pre-teen next met Max Hunter, folklore authority, while auditioning for a program of folk songs. His seventy recordings of Ozarkers singing traditional melodies, now housed in the Greene County Library, led her to the legendary Vance Randolph.

"Hunter and Randolph have the most important collections of Ozark folk songs," said Judy. "I'd check them out in high school and college. My college roommates could not see why I listened to these old people's crackly voices. So, I had to play the recordings when they were out of the room," recalled Domeny. "The songs grabbed me. I haven't veered from them."

Authenticity has become her trademark. "She hasn't 'blue-grassed' her songs or changed them to make the audience like them," said Gordon McCann, past president of the Missouri Folklore Society and consultant to the Smithsonian, National Geographic, and the National Endowment of the Arts. "She's made an honest effort to reenact songs that are part of our Ozark heritage."

On the family's eighty-five acre farm, Judy used the great outdoors to rehearse her stories' many verses. Learning to drive a tractor for hay haulers or picking rock required diversion, much like Ozark settlers needed. "Back then, they were plowing a field or scrubbing a washboard," said Judy. "They needed to take their mind off of what they were doing—at least for six or seven minutes."

Judy learned Hunter's "Deep Blue Sea," "The Drunkard's Child," "The Old Arm Chair," besides Randolph's "Down in the Willow Garden," and "The Red River Shore." She memorized the tales of the little blind child, a soldier's thoughts before battle, and suicidal heroines who die rather than live without true love. "There's a lot of silver daggers and lily-white breasts in these songs," she said.

Judy saves her most morose forty-five minutes for historical society presentations. Her melodic history lesson retells four real-life Missouri tragedies: "West Plains Explosion" mourns teenagers who were killed at a dance. "The Meek's Family Murder" centers around Nellie, who survived the massacre and burning of her parents and sister. "The Iron Mountain Baby" is the tale of an infant who was thrown off a train. "Resurrection Sunday" is a bizarre narrative about a son's attempt to bury his mother's frozen corpse.

"Her serious research of these little-known regional stories is a valuable service in preserving the tradition of balladry,"

McCann said.

"The sad songs make me cry initially, but once I get over that, they are just interesting," said Judy. She appreciates the beautiful and simple melodies. "They are my entertainments. I have pictures, like little movies, in my head. Some are in color and some in black and white."

That's rather like the rest of her life. While her songs chronicle the dark past, Judy's present splashes through primary colors. An art teacher at Willard South Elementary School, she's decorated her home with framed animal paintings her students created. The living room is dotted with a new hobby, creating four-inch ceramic scenes from family photographs.

Domeny's latest recording stems from a program of her own folk songs. Drawing on twelve years in education, Judy writes lightheartedly about faculty meetings, school cancellations, and February without recess. Her "So You Want to be a Teacher" advises would-be teachers to acquire a smile, a good bladder, psychic powers, "Band-Aids for the fingers," and "words to heal the soul."

Her after-school hours are taken with her parents' farm menagerie located a quarter mile up the road. Domeny and husband, David Bowen, promotions producer for KOLR-10 in Springfield, help with the cattle, horses, dogs, cats, and goats. He cuts wood; she chops ice and feeds the animals. "I cook better for them than I do for him. I have personal relationships with the dogs and goats," she said. "I should have been a professional petter."

Her love of animals incorporates into a Christmas program on the Nativity stable; another develops as listeners choose the songs by picking up toy animals. These hymns, patriotic, and favorite folk songs give balance to Domeny's preferred tales of woe.

"I'm careful when I mix them in now. At a folk festival, the real folk enthusiasts will be interested. The general population won't understand why I'm singing about death," said the Queen of Death and Dying. "As it is, I don't get invited to sing at many parties."

A Double Dose of Miracles
Chrissy St. Martin

Sometimes miracles come in small packages, and Chrissy St. Martin was due. 1998 was a plain bad-luck year for the Nixa, Missouri, teenager. In August, one of her pregnant mares died of colic. In September, her family's new house burned to the ground. Her gelding, spooked by a rabbit, bucked her off, and her foot caught in the stirrup. Her broken ankle required surgery and a cast for six weeks. Pancreatitis, the reoccurring side effect of her kidney transplant medications hospitalized Chrissy another four weeks.

"I imprinted them. I blew into their noses so they would know me, and I petted them and talked to them," said Chrissy St. Martin on teaching her twin foals to bond with her.

Then in May of 1999, her luck changed. Her six-year-old barrel racing quarter horse, Lady, foaled. And foaled again. "We never expected two," said Chrissy. "We got there just in time to see Lady stand up, and the Paint drop. While Dad was talking to our vet on the cell phone, he thought he saw another leg. Before she could get here, the sorrel's head popped out."

The foals' veterinarian, Dr. Ruth Massey, knew the deck was stacked against the twins. She estimates less than five percent of mares ever conceive twins. Producing two live, healthy babies is even rarer.

"This happens in only one out of every 10,000 births," said Massey. "Mares are not equipped for twins. Usually the larger fetus gets all the nutrition, and the smaller one starves to death. Then the mare will abort them both. These two foals were small but were very normal."

Still, the Paint, at only forty-five pounds was dismature. Christened Cashing in the Chips, he wore padded bandages to support his yet unossified knees and was kept penned to limit his exercise. Out-weighed and out-muscled by his brother at the teat, Chips was separated from his mother and put on mare's milk replacement. "We had to wean him at three days," said Massey, who kept a close eye on the foal during his tenuous first days. "Lady was pacing so much, he couldn't keep up with her. He started bowing out, so we took him away from her and raised him as an orphan."

Feeding him every three hours for five months was made easier by Chrissy's involvement. "I imprinted them," said Chrissy. "I blew in their noses so they would know me, and I petted and talked to them. We've had two other foals. It's easier for people to work on the babies if there is an emergency."

Near miniature versions of normal newborns, the twins weighed together about what one single-birth foal would. Like most babies, nursing and napping took up much of their time. After a few minutes suckling, the effort overcame them. They folded down to their knees and willingly plopped near Chrissy to doze off against her.

Small wonder. A willowy wisp of a girl, Chrissy bubbles over with laughter and good spirits. After all, she's beating the odds herself. At four years old, she lost both kidneys to Glomerulonephritis, a strep infection and received one of her mother's kidneys in 1989.

"Even when she first started talking, it was always horses, horses, horses," said her mother, Lonni St. Martin. "We had her wait until she was nine to start riding. She had to be careful with the kidney."

Reluctantly given the medical okay to cinch up, Chrissy started riding lessons. Others practicing barrel racing caught her attention. "My parents wouldn't let me on a horse too early," said Chrissy. "Each horse I've gotten has brought me up another level, so I've never been scared."

Chrissy learned the fundamentals on sweet-tempered Sugar. "She had bundles of patience," said Chrissy. "When I took spills doing barrels, she'd just stop and wait for me to get up and finish the pattern."

Chrissy's medication regimen, her half-hearted interest in piano lessons and basketball practice settled as dust behind her passion for horses. Saddling up her registered quarter horses, Kasman and Lady, Chrissy's competed in barrel racing, pole racing, and team penning since 1996. Goat tying is her newest interest. To do so, she gulps down thir-

teen pills daily to keep her kidney healthy. She weaves
through the chronic back pain and inescapable stomachaches
as determinedly as she does the barrels in the rodeo arena.
"You have to take a chance," she said of the transplant. "I've
lived my whole life with it, so I've adapted to it."

Feeding Chip complicated the St. Martin's already
crowded schedule. Kasman still requires trail rides and run-
throughs on pole and barrel courses, a walking distance from
the twins' enclosures. In Nixa, Chrissy and the horses normally head to team penning practices two or three times a
week. Another evening bites the dust when her dad takes
them for indoor arena practices in nearby towns. To compete
in ShoMe Horse Association, All Youth Rodeo Association,
and the Missouri Team Penning Association events, her
Friday-Saturday-Sunday itineraries crisscross the Ozarks.
Some weekends are two-event-two-town appearances to
build up points. She wears the rodeo shirt her mother sewed
for her and the first-place belt buckle she and Lady won in
1997 as high-point pair in barrel racing. Summer added
Lady's postpartum reconditioning. Chip's daytime feedings
remain Chrissy's responsibility. The after-dark and midnight
feedings fall to Dave St. Martin. When they're on the road, her
mother tends the horses.

"It's scary sometimes," said Lonni. "But, we feel like if we
told her she couldn't do anything, it'd be holding her back.
It's made her tough. You wouldn't know she's had a kidney
transplant if you just met her."

With a mouthful of braces and ears full of earrings, the
blue-eyed blonde does slip into glittery black dresses and
high heels for dances and good times with school pals, Sarah
and Megan. "They're my best friends," said Chrissy. "I was on

medicine that puffed me out like a little balloon, and they stuck by me. When our house burned down, they had a big party for us."

Chrissy St. Martin practices with a new mount in preparation for team penning competitions.

The electrical fire completely destroyed the St. Martin home in 1998. Chrissy and Dave were moving older sister, Nicole, into her college dorm at the time. Lonni, working in the basement, escaped with only the family dog.

"I lost photos of my friends and the ribbons and trophies that I've won in the past. They were not just about horses; they were memories," Chrissy said.

For now, she jumps in the saddle and never looks back. For team penning and pole competitions, Chrissy rides Kasman Chick who picked up a shiny belt buckle in poles himself during 1998. Reading books, watching videos, and talking with other people, Chrissy trained both the nine-year old to the poles and Lady to the barrels. "Kasman is a good pole horse," said Chrissy. "He can really move through the poles consistently. But he just loves team penning. He's totally focused, and it shows," said Chrissy. "Lady's showed promise on the barrels. She's had a 15.9 second finish after only three months training. Once we didn't know she sprained her ankle, and she ended up winning the race on three legs. She had enough heart to finish the race."

After a kicking injury ended her 1997 season, Lady (registered as Here's Looking At You All) was bred to Painted Cash Maker. Both horses descend from Dash for Cash, the legendary quarter horse stallion. The St. Martins hoped for an offspring with speed; Chrissy just wanted a Paint.

Lady's foals are a fifty-fifty mix. The largest one, You All Cashing In, was a thirty-two inch duplicate of his sorrel dam. Chips at twenty-nine inches, bore the coveted splash of white. Whatever abilities they develop–either in performance or show–the twins aren't for sale. Driving from their rented duplex to check them during torrential spring storms permanently bonded the St. Martins to the pair. Even Kasman adopted the Paint, watching over him during his early outings in the pasture.

"We're keeping them," Chrissy said. "When it comes time to get them trained, we'll figure out what they do best in. We could never sell them." The St. Martins can't sell Sugar, now retired to pasture, or Kasman, or Lady, or their yearlings, Bominos Stardust or Boogie Nights either.

The blueprint for rebuilding their home requires acreage large enough to accommodate their four-footed family members. Aspiring to equine college to become a horse trainer, Chrissy wants to attend a university close enough to keep tabs on Chips, his sorrel brother, and the rest of her menagerie.

"These are Lady's first babies," said Chrissy. "She's the only one who could have pulled this off. She's got a bunch of heart."

Maybe Lady isn't the only one.

The Face of Courage
Rodeo Clowns

In the rodeo arena, a lifetime lasts eight seconds, and bravery ends in nine. Poised at the tick of the clock, the man in baggy pants and lopsided smile waits. Under the greasepaint and the buffoonery, the rope tricks and the jokes, the rodeo clown stands in the dust as a profile in courage.

Now a Ph.d in English, Ken "Butch" Rose, once entered the rodeo arena by parachute. (Photo courtesy of Ken "Butch" Rose.)

July, 1999, nearly fifty rodeo clowns reunited at the Rodeo of the Ozarks in Springdale, Arkansas. Their experience stretches across the history of rodeo clowning. Some, now in their eighties and nineties, did everything—fed the stock, rode the horses, and lassoed a laugh from the crowd with an underwear joke.

Others return as modern-day specialists, distinguished as bullfighters or barrelmen.

"I see them as unsung heroes," said event organizer, Gail Woerner. "One minute they joked around with kids in the crowd; the next they were standing in front of a bull, saving a cowboy's life. My goal has been to see they are recognized before they are gone."

Since 1993, Woerner has been the ramrod of the biennial gathering of these senior citizens of slapstick. Initially their greasepaint got her. Helping rodeo clowns entertain underprivileged children, Werner discovered no comprehensive history of their career. Her research resulted in *Fearless Funnymen: the History of the Rodeo Clown*. She's been hooked ever since, writing newsletters, and scheduling their reunion for them.

Ninety-year-old Oregon resident, Monk Carden, clowned when the biggest danger in the arena was the audience's boredom. As old cows and steers were replaced by the Brahma, the rodeo's focus shifted, and so did the clown's roles. Fort Smith resident, Ken Boen, is another of those early pioneers. On the road a hundred days of the year, he rode bulls and then entertained between events with his menagerie of dogs, ducks, and trick horse, The Old Gray Mare. The act played in Madison Square Garden five years, earned mention in *Variety* and *Billboard*, and brought his future wife to him for an autograph.

"I loved it," said Lynn. "I was his chief cook and bottle washer. I never missed a show, except for the bulls. Then, I'd always have an excuse to take the horses around or water them or dry them off. I had a horrible thought of losing him."

Lynn had good reason to worry. On eye level with the Brahma, clowns protected the riders. Using only their agility and speed, their job was to divert the bull from a dismounting or fallen rider. They developed into two specialists—the bullfighter who runs for safety and the barrelman who dives into it.

Jimmy Schumacher, inventor of the "Walking Barrel," sits with Gail Woerner, reunion coordinator and author of Fearless Funnymen. (Photo courtesy of Gail Woerner.)

Bobby Clark, Cowboy Hall of Fame and ProRodeo Hall of Fame Inductee, found his preference early on. "I started in the barrels, but got out real quick," he said. "It put knots on my head."

He and his brother, Gene, returned to Springdale where they often performed during their thirty-year career. "That was always one of our favorite rodeos," Clark said. "We worked it many times. After the show, 'Shorty' Parsons would barbecue out at his house. We made a lot of friends I want to see again." He remembered a bull that crashed through a fence and fell into one of the box seats. "The bull fell over a little kid and hit a woman—crushed some of her ribs. Gene and I jerked the little kid out into the arena with us," said Bobby.

Forty-three year old veteran, Bob Courtney was a barrelman when he and his horse, Oxodol, weren't working the crowd for laughs. His barrel, now custom made, is not so far away from the first barrel Jasbo Fulkerson used. Unable to run long distances to the arena wall, the short-legged Fulkerson simply fitted automobile tires over the first clown barrel and painted it red. A decade later, when a bull poked its head in the barrel and got stuck, Jimmy Schumacher knocked out the other end for an escape route and patented the walking barrel.

Courtney's barrel is also open on both ends. Handles and padding inside protect him and foam rubber outside protects the bull from injury. "The scariest experience I had was when a bull hit the barrel running wide open. It broke the barrel's top ring, and I rolled end over end eight times. Then the bull pushed it thirty feet to the fence. It was the wildest ride I've ever had," he said.

Getting gored ripped, kicked, and trampled by an eighteen-hundred pound animal is secondary to the responsibilities in the arena. Rodeo clowns get their ribs split, their vertebrae crushed, their arms and legs snapped like sticks, and still they return. The reason why they do it weighs more than the stack of broken bones. It is simply their job. "I got run over a lot of times to keep somebody else from getting run over," said bullfighter Ken "Butch" Rose. "It's our job to protect that bull rider. I've been a bull rider myself, and I know how important a clown is to the bull rider's safety. When a bull rider jumps off or gets thrown off, he's at the bull's mercy. The clown gets between him and the bull."

"It's the adrenalin," explained Courtney. "It's the same reason race car drivers go fast. It's the push to see how far you can go without getting hurt."

The perils of the long horn and sharp hoof take their toll. Eventually, clowns wipe off the makeup and retire to more sedate professions. Ken and Lynn Boen settled in Fort Smith in 1951, putting horses through their tricks at church and youth camps and starting a Christian Cowboy Club.

Ken "Butch" Rose, with a doctorate degree in English, teaches at Branson's College of the Ozarks, performs in a band

Rodeo clowns relax between reunion events. Besides appearing in the stands and rodeo arena, they sign autographs, march in a parade, and visit area hospitals and nursing homes. (Photo courtesy of Gail Woerner.)

with his wife, and saddles up as an extra at Shepherd of the Hills Outdoor Theater. Bob Courtney settled in Sparta, Missouri, and was the first clown in Branson's Dixie Stampede Western Show. Retiring in 1978, Bobby Clark worked as a feed salesman, owned a 700-acre cattle ranch, and raised thoroughbreds near Warner, Oklahoma. Others sought jobs in commercial art, education, truck driving, bird dog training, retailing western wear, and law enforcement.

Woerner's 1999 reunion was the fourth event she's orchestrated for the retired clowns. Guthrie (OK), Sante Fe (NM), and Colorado Springs (CO) preceded the Springdale gathering. "When I did the book, I thought it was a onetime deal," she said. "But I got very connected with these people. Rodeo clowns have always been second-class citizens, portrayed as drunks who got hurt or can't do anything else. I realized that image was bogus. They are like the down-to-earth people I grew up with in Colorado."

Woerner's since written *Belly Full of Bedsprings*, a history of bronco riding. A third book focuses on bull riding's history. Between reunions, she corresponds by newsletter to the ry. Between reunions, she corresponds by newsletter to the men and works toward the next round up.

Springdale's event honored the retired clowns from fourteen states. For them, the reunion is a chance to visit friends about old times. Near the stands and fans again, they slip into their gaudy shirts and misshapen hats to sign autographs, ride in the parades, and help during the Exceptional Rodeo. There's something about the smell of grease paint and the roar of the crowd that draws the rodeo clown.

The Lights of
MARSHFIELD
AND
CONWAY

Ozarks Soul

I Think I'll Pass on Paradise

think I'll pass on Paradise—at least that heaven-on-earth variety. Some think Hawaii is as close to Paradise as this planet can offer. I've been there. Certainly it was nice. On Monday, the sun smiled down on me. The wind unraveled my hair and buffed away the rough edges worry had made. I walked out of the tepid, turquoise waters, and simply drip-dried, brushing white sand and salt from my too-tight skin. Then it rained. Broad- fringed banana and palm leaves fairly gleamed. And then on Tuesday, the sun smiled down on me. The wind unraveled

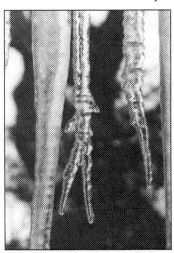

That year winter won. January's cruelty bowed the cedars. Ice, like frozen tears, hung from bayberry berries. (Photo by Gerald W. Dupy)

my hair and buffed out rough edges worry had made. The tepid water invited me in, and I drip dried, brushing white sand and granules of salt from my too-tight skin. Then it rained. The broad leaves shone again with Tuesday's slickness. And then on Wednesday, the sun smiled down on me in the bliss of predictable sameness.

But no, I think I'll pass on the Pacific's Paradise. I prefer the Plateau. Oh, it's hot in the Ozarks. Nothing can cook the brain faster than a withering July heat. It shimmers off hard surfaces. It scorches corn stalks. It shrinks hay to string. It chases the wind from the shade and turns it inside out. It dries grass into brown twigs, and scum forms greasy lids on quiet lakes. August's dog days suck the azure from the sky, and locusts screech in the trees.

Unquestionably, summer is an unrelenting assault. Sweat puddles in dark circles under our arms and at the waist. We water the flowers by hand, don wide-brimmed hats, and hurry through the shadowless light toward the fans. Just when we've found another seed tick, scratched one more chigger, squeezed the last blackberry sticker from the palm of our hand, the heat releases us from its fiery grip. The respite is exquisite.

The sky returns to sapphire. The clouds whiten and billow again. The air, once strung out in a thin, gray haze, clears and crisps. The adoration the sun once tried to force from unbending hills is now given freely. Mountain peaks raise a mighty "Hallelujah!" to autumn. Trees that nearly fainted in the heat, sing a song of colors. Their canon builds on the deep, rich browns of blackjack and pin oak. Contrapuntal melodies meander through the under story in sumac and sassafras, back lit like cathedral glass.

And then there is the hickory. Like a sentinel at our front yard entrance, one stood on guard with a limestone rock big enough for three to sit on. Shells littered the ground, harvested and discarded by bushy-tailed squirrels. On one particular October day, a breeze stirred from the southwest field and wafted over the pond and toward the barn. The hickory, as if unable to stand one more second of beauty, sighed. Its leaves, en masse, fell silently like golden rain. Alas, winter.

It couldn't be Paradise without winter. The bite of the wind, the snapping of twigs half hidden in the grass prelude what's to come. November drapes its gauzy curtains around the Plateau. It clings to bark and plasters fallen leaves into ditches and eaves. To prepare, we caulk the cracks, count the wood by rows, and lock the windows tight.

Winter is a wicked adversary. One Christmas morning, we planned to escape its wind and drifts, intending to open our presents on the farm and then drive to the Illinois grandparents for turkey dinner. We loaded suitcases, fruitcake, and the kids into the station wagon and headed toward the main road. Unfortunately, the sun had merely softened the snow on the big hill between the house and the blacktop. Just short of completely melting, the snow on our lane had become a veneer of ice that only tow trucks could manage. And they weren't running on Christmas.

That year, winter won. Christmas dinner was chicken noodle soup and crackers. The fireplace glass cracked four times from the fires we had built, defending ourselves from the windy chill. We tore up the utility room floor and trenched the water lines, searching for frozen pipes.

Bringing in the New Year, January's cruelty bows the cedars. Ice, like frozen tears, hangs from bayberry berries.

Just as winters terrors seem unending, winter claims its victory and moves on. The snow melts. Redbud and wild plum line the creek beds. Dogwood powders the hills with white. Forsythia and spirea fling their blossoms in exultation, their fragile petals twirling like confetti in the fresh, spring air. Calves on wobbly legs shadow their mothers in the fields. The pinks deepen to red in the fire bush and tulips. The green ripens to emerald, and honeysuckle's tawny scent lingers by the road. The rains come. Some fall softly like invitations to the dance. Others pound tender seedlings and drown river bottom fields.

Then it gets hot. There's nothing like an Ozark summer. By the Fourth of July, tomatoes hang like ruby goblets on the vine. The heat withers and parches and boils and bakes. It swelters and clings like a sweaty lover to our skins. We sigh, both repelled and seduced by it.

I think I'll pass on travel-poster bliss. To me, Paradise is in the search, the dread, the anticipation, the experience, the challenge, the loss, and the relief from change. Before I get to heaven, I'll take the glorious mutations of the very air—here, on the Ozark Plateau.

Bedding Down in History
The Dickey House

"Sooner or later, just about everyone uses the Dickey House," said Bill Buegsen. It hosts weddings, fashion shows, board and church meetings, plays, and dinner parties.

Beyond the Carnegie library, steepled churches, and a rickety crossing over the railroad tracks, an eloquent reminder of the past resides. Azaleas, holly bushes, an aviary, and gazebo landscape the lawn where young ladies in sunbonnets and voile dresses might have sipped lemonade. Massive oaks circling the walk and white antebellum columns guard the entrance, like stately soldiers, against the indiscreet. Welcome to the Dickey House.

Two stories tall and filling a block of Clay Street, the structure dwarfs residences and rivals even the Webster County Courthouse. It overshadows the billboards chronicling Marshfield's often-crowned basketball teams and store windows stenciled with long-established family names.

Sam Dickey, former oxen driver and son of a hanged Confederate sympathizer, followed his mother and sister to the quiet town twenty miles east of Springfield in 1870. Studying to be a doctor and a druggist, Dickey finally settled on a law career, and as the town developed, he became the prosecuting attorney. He contracted the eight-room mansion for his family in 1913 with five thousand dollars from his successful defense of a Springfield boxer.

Eighty years later, after the last of the family and a succession of short-term owners abandoned it, the Dickey House was rescued from the musty smell of disrepair. William and Dorothy Buesgen recognized the beauty that lay just under the peeling paint and cracking wallpaper. In a labor of love, they restored the building's prominence in the community, creating a retirement business for themselves.

Owners of the Dickey House since 1989, the Buesgens are not native Ozarkers. They never intended to relocate here nor renovate a four-thousand square foot building. Heading to Dorothy's sister in New Jersey, they accidentally bumped into the Show-Me state.

"I wanted to avoid the Ozarks at all costs," recalled Bill, "because of 'The Beverly Hillbillies.' But when we came to the Missouri border, I fell in love. It reminded me of Germany where I was born."

Altering their vacation plans, the Buesgens stayed to explore Springfield's back roads and outlying communities.

"Everywhere we stopped, people were so nice," he said. "They were always waving at us. It was totally different from California. We drove through Marshfield, and suddenly we found this place. It was as if the house had been calling us. Dorothy turned to me and said, 'I think we've found home.'"

The Buesgens quickly contacted the agent in charge of the house, and twenty-four hours later they purchased it.

"Actually, people thought we would just bulldoze it down," Bill said. Though structurally sound, the Dickey House had been empty for three years. The plaster ceilings bowed. Five layers of wallpaper rippled across the walls. Wood casings, holding the sliding parlor doors, had separated. The shag carpet was matted beyond raking.

The upgrade took eighteen months. The couple shuttled between the Marshfield project and Bill's contracting obligations in Redondo Beach. Eventually Dorothy moved in. Bill returned every six weeks, bringing truckloads of fencing and European antiques. They turned the eight hundred square foot attic into their living quarters. On the second floor, he added more bathrooms for the proposed bed and breakfast clientele. He repositioned doors and created false fireplaces to camouflage the effort. On the ground level, they remodeled the kitchen, removed the carpet, refinished the inlaid wood floors and put on a fresh layer of plaster. They built a backyard cottage, housing the Garden Suite and the Queen Anne Suite. Their Roman and Victorian decors include double Jacuzzis, gas fireplace, cable TV, and laundry facilities.

The renovation finished, Bill and Dorothy decorated the Dickey House with personal possessions. In the living room, portraits of the Buesgen's three children sit on the piano. Egyptian statues, trophies from Bill's Arabian horses, stand near the living room fireplace. A gilt-framed heirloom land-scape hangs above the mantle. The Russian wild boar, the ten-point deer, and a five-pound bass hang in the den.

Dorothy made the dining room drapes from red velvet and created living room curtains from fifty-four yards of chintz and moire fabric. "We couldn't find anything long enough unless it was custom made. The panels had to be ten feet long, so we decided to make them ourselves," she said.

"I told Bill, 'You're going to have to help me.' He made yards and yards of trim. It took a week to make the first drape. Then we made the other three in five days."

The bedroom motifs also come from Dorothy's machine. Matching dust ruffles, pillows, and tablecloths swathe the Bouquet Room with blue and yellow, the Springtime Room with green, and the Fontaine Room in soft mauve. Bill built the canopy which tops the four poster Rice bed in the Heritage Room and the Roman columns which frame the Garden Suite's hot tub.

Old World elegance embellishes each room. Rich mahogany curls in ornate carvings over armchairs and sofa backs. The dining room buffet reaches to twelve-foot ceilings. Lion heads guard the doors of the Belgium antique. The silver service and individual napkin rings complement Dorothy's own pumpkin pancakes, apple cider, and turnovers. "It's real Victorian," said Bill. "Dottie enjoys doing it."

Dorothy readily agreed. "I do all the dishes. Bill does the serving. We're really a team."

The Dickey House bed and breakfast business thrives. Bill estimates five hundred visitors stay over night each year in the triple-diamond facility. A little more than an hour from

Dorothy and Bill Buegsen stand in front of a portrait of "Miss Ella" Dickey, whose historic mansion the California couple restored as a bed and breakfast inn.

Branson and three hours out of St. Louis, it has sheltered guests from thirty-seven states.

Beyond the tourist trade, the Buesgen's have returned the house to the Marshfield's community. Ella Dickey was the last of her family to live in the house. During the fifty years she lived in her childhood home, the mansion was a bright spot to the community. She decorated it lavishly during the holidays and provided a home-away-from-home for farm youngsters attending school in town.

"She was always extremely nice to the children," Dorothy recalled of the spinster who managed the town library for a half century. "She made Halloween a special event. Ghosts in the attic would slide on a rope. Eyes would peer out from everywhere."

"Miss Ella's manger scene on the upstairs balcony frequently won the Christmas decorating contest," Miles Hudson recalled. Over a half century ago, he boarded with Miss Ella because he had no transportation for the nineteen miles between his farm and high school. He traded household chores for an upstairs room and breakfast in front of the cook stove with Miss Ella.

The Buesgen's collect information about their house. They have copies of newspaper articles, legal documents, and historical pamphlets concerning the house and the family. They found *The Lamplighter: An Orphan Girl's Struggles and Triumphs* signed by Ella's mother, December 25, 1908. Portraits of Ella and Sam hang in the hall foyer.

Today, the Dickey House is used as a grand backdrop for special events. The high school drama department performed "Christmas Past, Present and Future," with Scrooge, Mrs. Cratchet and Tiny Tim performing throughout the house. The townspeople dropped by for open house and cookies.

The staircase and fireplace, the gazebo, and front steps backdrop brides in lace and antique satin. One couple, Civil War enthusiasts, dressed in Antebellum skirts and Confederate uniforms for their outdoor wedding. The mansion's living room and dining room were decorated for the reception.

"Sooner or later just about everyone uses the Dickey House for a party or get-together," Bill said. "It goes on all year."

The Gideons, women clubs, school administrators, members of the Webster Electric Co-op, or the convalescent hospital regularly make Dorothy's luncheon menu the centerpiece of their meetings. Area churches reserve the living room for holiday festivities or receptions.

"People come by and just sit down in the garden," said Bill. "The first thing visitors do is come see the Dickey House. We always let them."

This open-door policy is easy for the Buesgens. Marshfield personifies the best of rural small towns. The Buesgens have no qualms about running personal errands even when their establishment is full of people.

"When we left for California in January 1991, we forgot to lock the door. It was open for three days. But nobody came in. Everything was as it is now. That's the kind of people we have here," said Bill. "It's not hard to give back to the community when they have been so good to us," he said.

Past the front hall's suit of armor, the ambiance at 331 Clay Street is not hard to define. The house that Dickey built and the home that Buesgens created combine for sleep or celebration—for the Marshfield community and the passerby.

Children Read Living Textbooks
The Secret Garden

Hidden between two wings of Hubble Elementary School grows a Secret Garden. Over the wooden bridge and by its winding brick path, pansies flower in the spring. Pumpkins and mums thrive in the fall. The outdoor classroom, with its butterfly garden, teepee, pond, plants, and live-in wildlife, has become a living textbook for Marshfield's primary students.

The pussy willow that students planted in the spring bloomed into several lessons. In science, first graders watched its life cycle through furry-flower and yellow-pollen stages. "It's such a tactile plant. The students related well to it,"

Handprints on the teepee declare a visual roll call of students who use The Secred Garden. (Photo by J.P. Liang, Springfield (Mo.) News-Leader.)

said their teacher, Cheryl Willis. In language and art activities, the plant inspired reading "The Willow Cats" and "The Pussy Willow", and they illustrated the poems with puffed-wheat on construction paper.

"They bring in every turtle they find to the Secret Garden," said Willis. "When we went outside to read, the kids discovered two still hibernating. All they could see of one was its shell."

The Secret Garden project blossomed in spite of tight-money educational budgets. The idea for the garden was rooted in the town. "Although schools talk about involving the community, it's often hard to do," said Virginia Ahrens, the project's start-up coordinator. "But here, it was like 'A Field of Dreams.' If you build it, they will come. People got involved."

Once, "The Bullpen" was a useless enclosure overrun by Bermuda grass. A few trees, a transformer, and satellite dish stood in the tangle of weeds. Then Ahrens, longtime second-grade teacher, grafted two suggestions together.

"The retired teachers' association was looking for a project, and one of our teachers kept suggesting we do something with the courtyard," recalled Ahrens.

Ahrens asked the teachers' planning committee for ways to improve the area. Their on-the-spot recommendation was to build a bridge over the shallow drainage ditch that dissected the spot.

The idea germinated under research on outdoor classrooms until Terri Bitting, then technician with the Webster County Soil and Water Conservation District, provided the catalyst. "Terri had vision," said Ahrens. "She said it needed a path. That was the key."

Bitting sketched a path, beginning with a bridge and winding through the sixty by hundred ninety-foot area. Its loops and curves would create individualized learning spaces. The faculty liked the concept. The Board of Education liked it, until it came to funding.

"The attitude of the Board was simple. 'You have our blessing to do anything you like, but you just can't have any of our money,'" said Ahrens. "One year I tried to sneak cement and lumber into my classroom budget, but, of course, that didn't work."

Seed money did come from the sale of five hundred "Secret Garden" tee-shirts and coloring books. Then word got around. Ahrens spoke to the Rotarians, Optimists, and the Garden Club, whose donations purchased grass killer and lumber.

"I'd listen to suggestions and match them up with some-one else. Sometimes I'd tell the story, and friends would just hand me money," she said.

Wal-Mart contributed seeds, trees, and decorative rock; McDonald's donated a sundial. Hampton's Greenhouse supplied a birdbath. Webster Electric provided the fencing around the electrical transformer. Biggs Rock Quarry furnished pea gravel.

The children, kindergarten through third grade, suggested over a hundred names for the area and then chose "The Secret Garden." Meanwhile, a transformation was developing just outside their windows.

"Diversity brought life back into that area," said Bitting. "Once we got rid of the monoculture, little grasses, and weeds, foxtail grew up. That brought the bees and insects. The bees and insects brought the birds. That created a natur-

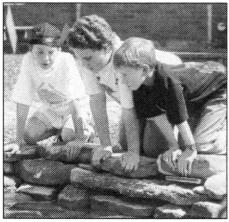

Science class convenes over the pond at Hubble Elementary School as students look for salamanders. (Photo by J.P. Liang, Springfield (Mo.) News-Leader.)

al bird feed area behind the cedar stumps."

Inside, Ahrens' class saw the whole thing. "One day one of my kids said, 'Boy, it sure is noisy out there.' Insects and birds had flocked in. It was great."

Meanwhile, the community began contributing what Ahrens calls "sweat equity." People from all economic levels and the students themselves got involved. Volunteers began digging the path by hand. When its wood chips floated away with spring rains, the junior high Environmental Club, schooled too far away to use The Secret Garden themselves, dug twenty-four hundred bricks out of a Bolivar landfill for the project. Cub Scout Den #2 scooped out the eight by fifteen pond and made birdhouses. The Campfire Girls built a mound for a teepee. A second grade class planted wildflowers to attract butterflies. Jerry Wonder built six picnic tables with lumber bought by the Parent-Teacher Support Group. Kenneth George installed electrical outlets at the arbor. Volunteers placed the bricks in a herringbone pattern, sometimes working in the dark. Others donated posts for flower boxes, four tons of rock for the tiered pond, boards for a split-rail fence, and sand.

"One couple made a forty-mile round trip just to get

goat manure. It doesn't smell," said Ahrens. "The kids put wood pulp in the bottom of a flowerbed, and we mixed in the goat manure. I had my class plant flower seeds and tomato plants. They grew like mad."

Tom Bitting, part Cherokee Indian, and two other native Americans, provided a twelve-foot teepee. At its dedication ceremony, Bitting dressed in buckskins to bless the students and the structure. Seven hundred fifty children painted their handprints on the teepee to become part of the Secret Garden.

"Then something unexpected happened," recounted Ahrens. "Memorials we didn't plan on started coming in." A wooden bench, a red twig dogwood, redbud, and fruit trees honoring a longtime educator, a custodian, and three school-age accident victims became part of The Secret Garden.

In all, the material donations and volunteered time created a project valued at forty-five hundred dollars for about six hundred dollars.

Officially dedicated in May 1996, the outdoor classroom continues as a work-in-progress. It has yet to acquire its flagpole, weather station, telescope, prairie grass, and other native trees. Discovering more ways to incorporate the outdoor classrooms in the learning process is a project goal. Volunteers hope similar sites can be developed for the fourth through sixth graders and at the junior high.

Still, children don't need future perfection. They have bonded to the project tighter than beggars lice to socks. "The kids couldn't be more helpful," Willis said. "They weed. They rake. They carry things to the compost pile. Every grandparent in town gets pulled outside to the The Secret Garden on Grandparents' Day."

"In the spring, we planted pumpkins," said Willis. "Then in the fall we saw the vines, the flower, the young and ripened fruit, the mature pumpkin. When they cut them open, they saw the seeds for the next year's pumpkins and counted them. They pulled out the seeds. They squealed, 'This is gross. Can I do it again?' Some picked their pumpkins, then weighed and measured them. That was good math."

Spring weather draws classes to check last year's mint and strawberries or find toad eggs in their jelly string. They sit at the tables to write or draw in the sunshine. Young readers pair off on the benches to share a book. At-risk volunteers talk with students there. Science lessons may be as large as studying the rebirth of an ecosystem or as small as watching the creepy-crawlies under cedar logs. That's one kind of fine print Hubble Elementary students like reading.

Ladies in Landscaping
Char Fox and Terri Bitting

erri Bitting and Char Fox work with rock and hard places. Partners in Ladies in Landscaping, the friends step into overalls, pick up the wheelbarrow, and head for the great outdoors. If not mountains, they certainly move rock, tons of it. They position dump trucks full of soil, plant trees and flowers for Springfield, Marshfield, Strafford, and Fair Grove lawns.

"You wouldn't want to wear the same dress to a dinner party,"

Terri Bitting and Char Fox arrange the finishing touches on a Springfield customer's backyard waterfall. "We don't work harder; we work smarter now," says Bitting. "Seventy-five percent of what we do is very hard work."

Char explained of the philosophy they plant with their phlox. "So why should the outside of houses look alike?"

Disdaining the oft-repeated red-barberry-yellow-yew shrubbery, they begin with the clients themselves. "From a woman's standpoint, we offer a little more intimate understanding of what the client wants. We look at the yard and ask questions that we would want asked. We take the time to listen to the answers."

Ladies in Landscaping divide responsibilities during the initial consultation with house owners. Terri measures the yard and looks over the topography; Char talks with the clients. "I want to know where their mind is—where their heart is. Do they have kids or a dog that will be getting into the landscape? Will older people be using the area? What colors do they like? Do they like cut flowers? Would they like to grow herbs to cook with?"

From those beginning responses, the women create an exterior expression of their client's interior self. For some, they snag childhood memories of the blackberry patch behind the barn. For those who enjoy birds, they plant flowers that will attract hummingbirds.

One woman came to Bitting and Fox with a backyard crowded with problems. The eighteen by thirty-eight foot area was deteriorating with erosion. The steep slope was a nightmare to mow. Her attempt to display primitive antiques was dismal.

Bitting and Fox dug in. Their goal was to solve the logistics problem and give the client an English garden setting best suited for her antiques and part time gardening interests. They removed the grass, built levels, and winding paths. They laid a rock entrance up the slope and placed a ship's dinner bell and water pump among the yellows, purples, and whites they planted.

For another family with a taste for western decor, Bitting and Fox planted red twig redbuds, repositioned the family's wagon wheel, and defined the area by a split rail fence. The result—Colorado in a corner.

The two women (in business since 1994) met while volunteering at Marshfield's Hubble Elementary School. For Bitting, creating an outdoor classroom for the school was a transformational experience. Though her degree at Southwest Missouri State University is in horticulture, she worked six years for the Webster County Soil and Water, helping customers plan grazing systems and pasture management. Designing the children's classroom, she realized a long dormant need to get down and dirty again.

"I always wanted to be an artist, but I couldn't draw or do pottery. Then I realized landscaping was my canvas. The dirt is my clay. The rocks are my jewels. The flowers and plants are my paint," she said.

She struck out on her own. Her first job came after a plant party, patterned after the time-honored Tupperware gathering. Digging up a sixty-foot iris bed in Missouri's summer tested her resolve. "Thinning the plants, I thought, 'What have I done? I really like this work, but this is toiling labor. Who else would ever work with me?'"

Char Fox, a landscaping architect major and enthusiastic volunteer for the outdoor classroom seemed a natural. Agreeing in business philosophy, both insist on working the job themselves rather than hiring others. If there's a six-ton rock wall to build, Char starts at one end, and Terri starts at the other.

"We laugh a lot," confessed Char. "For me, that's the key. We have to have fun and make light of things in the real environment."

Though the business is firmly planted in the fiscal black, the two women have no desire to expand. For one thing, their families receive top priority. "We help our family and husbands get off to work or school, and we're home when they come back," said Terri. "One reason we work for ourselves is so we can provide income and control our own hours."

Middle-schooler Travis Bitting rides horses in 4-H and plays summer baseball. Char's teenage daughter, Jamie, competes in the United States Volleyball Junior League, and her mother follows her through the tournament circuit.

Ladies in Landscaping also want to establish its trademark. To work multiple projects in subdivisions would require repetitive, bush-in-a-bucket, bush-in-a-hole presentations. "We want to develop our niche. We want people who like our style for being different," said Char.

Though they never wilt under the demands of outdoor work, three years and one hundred fifty jobs have forced them to face physical limitations. "We don't work harder; we work smarter now," said Terri. "Seventy-five percent of what we do is very hard work. Moving dirt is hard work. The last part is the planting and the beautifying. It's the whole process, not just the end result. We pace ourselves. We give ourselves the time."

Although the ladies pride themselves on doing the complete job themselves, sometimes they need a helping hand. For moving large rocks and pulling out stumps, they hire men with bigger equipment. Conway residents, Becky Clevenger and Cheree Brown, adept with cement and laying rock walls, often help out. "We are so fortunate," said Terri. "One criteria for this business is that we get to work outside. We get to be a part of the sun, the rain, the wind, and the cold. Nature sustains us."

When the fingernail-breaking work is done, when the flowers are planted and in bloom, the women in Ladies in Landscaping step back. "What we do is offer people an invitation to get back out in nature, to become intimate with nature," said Terri. "The greatest satisfaction is people coming to appreciate what nature has to offer them in the first place."

Collector Turns to Stone
Willis Ezard

Conversation with Willis J. Ezard always turns to stone—amethystine, quartz, tourmaline, topaz, and agate. "I'm pretty thrilled with my rock collection," said the Conway resident. "If I see someone I say, 'Come by and see us, and I'll show you my rocks.'"

Ezard has filled shelves, tables, buckets, prescription bottles, and plastic bags with his sixty-five-year-old hobby. Large geodes, quartz, and petrified wood are piled on his workshop floor and spill

For over half a century, Willis J. Ezard of Conway has collected rocks from five continents. Some specimens are like old friends. (Photo courtesy of Bittersweet, Inc.)

outside into rock gardens.

Although the collection is almost uncountable, Ezard regards particular specimens like old friends. In just moments he can find a small piece he bought at Hell's Half Acre at Powder River, Wyoming. "My rock collection started when I paid twenty-five cents a piece for some petrified wood and moss agate," he recalled.

Since that 1936 beginning, he's traveled five continents panning, sifting, digging, and buying little bits of the world. Until his retirement as Conway school superintendent, Ezard's excursions were confined to summer vacations. Since his retirement, he travels when and where the *Lapidary Journal* beckons.

"The magazine is the source of my information about where rocks are located," Ezard said. After reading the *Journal*, Ezard and his wife hunted in Montana for sapphires, in North Carolina for rubies, in New Mexico for amethystine quartz, and in Tunder Bay, Ontario for amethysts. Closer to home, Ezard searched for the petal-shaped Barite Rose. The reddish rock is found only in a five-square-mile area at Norman, Oklahoma. His collection now includes golf ball to cabbage size roses.

Ezard said the satisfaction he derives from his rock specimens is threefold. "Mainly, they are beautiful," he said. "But there's the anticipation of what I'll find and the reward of actually digging out the material." Though Ezard said he is first a collector of rocks, he does fashion the raw rubies, sapphires, and quartz he has found into jewelry for his family and friends. He's designed an amethyst ring for himself, opal, turquoise, and topaz necklaces for his wife and daughter.

Using the faceting machine, a retirement present from the Conway community and faculty, Ezard follows precise charts for shaping the stones. He's cut one hundred seventy-eight facets in a golden topaz and one hundred, twenty-eight facets into a three-carat Brazilian topaz. Grinding the facets took nearly twenty-four hours.

"You don't want to make a mistake," he said. "If you do, you have to start all over again reshaping the stone."

Ezard's rocks mark many of the couple's travels. His collection includes a deposit from Old Faithful, alabaster from Egypt, granite from Mount Rushmore, and stones from the Sea of Galilee.

"My luggage was getting pretty heavy by the time we got home," Ezard said of the Holy Land trip. He has a chip off Mars Hill where Paul preached, an Eliat, the official gemstone of Israel, some marble from a synagogue in Capernaum, and a stone from the Acropolis in Athens.

"It's not just to say I've been there," Ezard explained. "The rock has to have some significance." Not convinced whether or not the Egyptians used quarried stone or man-made blocks to fashion the pyramids, Ezard brought back a chip from the Pyramid Cheops and sent it to the University of Missouri for analysis.

"We went to the Valley of Elah where David fought Goliath. We went to the brook where David got his five smooth stones. I picked up five smooth stones myself. Maybe they're some David picked up. He only used one, you know."

So well known is Ezard's love of rocks that friends sometimes bring them back to him from their travels. He obtained a sample of rare Turkish meerschaum rock that way.

"They've become personal," Ezard said of his Apache tears, lapis lazuli, smoky quartz, and crystal quartz. "You've sweated and gotten thirsty to get them. You've worked with them and shown them and talked about them."

Outdoor Greeting Cards
The Den of
Metal Arts

They're Christmas cards, and valentines, and Halloween jokes. Only they glow in the dark, glitter with garland, and stand twenty-two feet tall.

Their creator, Richard Kerb, calls his rooftop and yard figures silhouettes. To the passerby, cruising Interstate 44, near Conway's exit 113, the flags, cats, angels, holly, and hearts are oversize holiday fun. That's exactly why the Den of Metal Arts expanded from wrought iron railings and staircases to yard deco-

Every holiday gets its own marquee at the Den of Metal Arts.

rations in the first place. Kerb hoped his giant greeting cards would break the monotony of interstate travel with a little levity.

"We got into silhouettes strictly by accident," Kerb said. "I felt for the truck drivers who drove by at night. I thought if I put some lights up, they'd know it was just another twenty miles to the next rest stop. So we put a pumpkin between two witches and lighted them."

Truck drivers loved them. Three months later, Kerb had made six Christmas forms, including Santa in a train. Since then, his designs include Ol' Saint Nick on water skiis, in a speedboat, in a 1957 Chevy convertible, and driving a tractor. "Wreaths, the three-piece manger scene, and Santa with reindeer are our best sellers," Kerb said. "It spreads out from there."

And spread out it did. His part-time metalworking began in Conway, expanding to the frontage property just east of the Conway exit. His initial sixty by sixty structure there enlarged into thirty-two thousand square feet. His after-hours hobby became a full-time job manufacturing four hundred designs.

Inside the warehouse, designs cover eight thousand, five hundred square feet of showroom floor and walls. Walking through five warehouse rooms of candy canes, leprechauns, flags, Uncle Sam, ghosts, and pilgrims is like wandering through a giant calendar. Outside, carolers, dragons, stage-coaches, and semi-trucks light up over two thousand feet of the frontage road. With nearly nine million cars passing by on Interstate 44 in a year, his fairy tale pumpkins, sham-rocks, and hearts are the only advertising Kerb needs. Seventy-five percent of his business are drop-in vacationers.

"Most people drive by during the summertime in small vehicles and then come back later to pick up their order. We probably bring three thousand people to Branson that way. They go see a few shows, come back here on Sunday for their silhouette, and then drive ten to twelve hours back home." Traditional

Judy and Richard Kerb stand under a holiday yard ornament, one of the 400 wrought iron designs.

wrought iron filigree, spiral staircases, cemetery signs, and farm logos fill out the inventory. "We're willing to build anything," said Kerb of his five-person crew. "We've done both an airplane and a parachute. My son drew out a helicopter we developed."

Ideas come from any source. Some begin with customers' suggestions. The bucking bronco, cactus, and a dozen other western symbols came from customer requests. So did the Star of David and a Menorah.

"Richard saw a Christmas card and liked it so well we made it into a carriage silhouettes with fox trotters," said Judy Kerb. "People say their feet positions are just right. It's been real popular."

A three-dimensional Christmas tree, an elf boot, an oversized snowman, and a hummingbird with a flower are best viewed from a sixty-foot distance, the recommended space between the yard ornament and those who pass by.

Kerb also builds moving units—jumping reindeer, leaping frogs, a pirouetting ballerina, or walking camels. But he focuses on an uncomplicated ornament for most homeowners. "We looked at average individuals and made our unit so simple all they have to do is plug it in themselves," said Kerb. "They don't need an electrician to come out." To qualify for the "Handmade in the Ozarks" label, his wrought iron creations are created by hand, once the power machinery cuts the twenty-foot rods into specified pattern. The operator then shapes the pieces by bending them over dies. The welds are sculptured into the product, not just welded. Support bars strengthen each project, just in case a Missouri winter piles on more than sixty pounds of snow and ice.

Once the ornament has its form, Kerb's wife, Judy, wraps the silhouettes in Christmas lights and shiny garland. She positions each bulb with floral and electrical tape. The peak season is from April to mid-December. "I enjoy doing it," she said. "My best time is at night when there are no customers. There's never a dull moment during the day."

"My dream for these metal sculptures was to reach all the states," said Kerb. "When we finally wrote down all their locations, they had gone to all fifty states and five foreign countries in just five years. I reached my stars and didn't know it."

The Lights of

BUFFALO, BENNETT SPRING, AND NEVADA

The Firecracker Lady of Missouri
Jane Hale

When the red rockets glare and bombs burst midair, Jane Hale couldn't be happier. A big bash on the Fourth means another successful year for her family's fireworks business. When she's not selling sportswear or running beauty pageants, writing a newspaper column, or researching a novel, this silver-haired grandmother is busy

supervising Hale Fireworks, one of the country's five largest fireworks wholesalers.

"It's just like cooking ten pots of beans on the stove," said Jane. "You just find the one that's boiling

Jane Hale began her fireworks company with a roadside stand outside her Buffalo, Missouri home. Today, Hale Fireworks lights the skies from Iowa to the Gulf of Mexico. "We'll give you a Hale of a deal," she says.

and stir it."

Most weekends she cooks more than beans. Some Sundays require hot biscuits and mashed potatoes with gravy. Others spread out with Swiss steak or ham for a big dinner at the family farm near Buffalo, Missouri—except during firecracker season.

From Memorial Day to mid-July, Missouri's Firecracker Lady is too busy to cook. Of course, her husband, sons, daughters-in-law, and grandchildren wouldn't come anyway. The business, which supplies three hundred wholesalers and three hundred fifty retail outlets in six states, is a family affair.

Her husband, Bob, oversees the purchase and delivery of fireworks from China and Taiwan and supervises employees at their Buffalo headquarters. Rick, the eldest son, runs outlets in Mississippi and Louisiana. Reggie and his wife oversee Rainbow/Hale's Fireworks in Bentonville, Arkansas. Lucas, the youngest son, is on the road setting up fireworks tents. Mitchell, a partner with his parents, oversees operations that spread from Nebraska to the Gulf. Mitch's wife, Suzyn, manages two St. Charles locations and helps Jane with the mountain of paperwork.

For the Hale matriarch, ground zero is her at-home office three miles outside town. Wall-to-wall file cabinets keep color-coded folders filled with regulations about pyrotechnics. The statistics overflow into plastic crates and three computers where she files each independent contractor's state permits, county ordinances, and fire and safety licenses. She writes and records insurance, makes price lists, and computes each state's sales tax. All phone lines ring at her desk.

"If I'm in charge of something, I want to know every

detail," Jane said. It's been that way since the local dime store sold cherry bombs and silver salutes and Jane's mother, Inez Shewmaker, set up a small display between the gas station and Shewmaker's Auto Parts. As her grandsons needed summer projects, Inez suggested that Jane take over the stand.

"Every Fourth of July, my friends would drive by and wave, 'Hi there, Jane. We see you're selling fireworks again.' They'd laugh. They just thought it was some rinky-dink little operation."

Then Jane smiles slyly. "But, every year we traded cars."

She moved the stand into the station tire room, then outside city limits to the Dairy Queen and other service stations. As inventory increased and city restrictions expanded, she warehoused her fireworks in her basement, garage, and an empty dairy barn on the Hale farm.

The business grew. Her husband, already on the road as livestock dealer, suggested that she also sell fireworks wholesale. After joining the business in 1980, Mitchell suggested developing Christmas and New Year celebrations into a second fireworks season in the South.

Although business booms, the firecracker business is not Jane's only interest. For two decades, she's handled Miss Dallas County and Little Miss Dallas County Beauty Pageants. She operates Hale's Sportswear, which merchandises sports uniforms, equipment, and clothing for the town of 2,300. A lifelong Buffalo resident, Jane organizes fundraisers and compiles the high school alumni correspondence.

After triple bypass surgery in 1992, Jane pursued a long dormant interest in writing. She's working on two novels, writing and researching between fireworks phone calls or in the quiet before dawn. She writes a weekly newspaper column entitled "Little Jane Shewmaker...Buffalo As I Remember It" for the *County Courier*. Her poetry has been included in national anthologies, and her children's and historical short stories have won awards. She co-authored and published *Wonderland* with grandson, Nick in 1997. It has become the first in a series of middle-school mysteries.

"If I can develop my own career in writing and keep up my end of the businesses and family life, I feel like I've accomplished something," she said.

Still, when summer heats up around the Fourth, Jane turns her full attention to the fireworks business. In the showroom of their headquarters on Highway 65, the Hales display more than a thousand items.

Family firecracker labels also include "Hale Bomb" fire-crackers, "Hale's Mad Dog," "Hale's a Crackin'" multi-shells, and "Super Luke," an artillery shell. "Whistlin' Nick," a bot-tle rocket, is named for Mitch's son. In 1997, "Hale Bob" was born, a display shell that tails off like the comet, Hale-Bopp.

"Fireworks are as safe as the person who shoots them," Jane advises customers who keep business too brisk for cal-culating on the computer.

"We either count up the merchandise mentally or write it on the side of a sack," said Jane. "Mitch and Bob add it up in their heads, but I write it all down. When it's totaled, everything's on the sack."

The Hales don't celebrate on the Fourth of July, since it's their largest retail sales day. Once the smoke clears and receipts funnel in, the Hales store their tents and shrink-wrap loose merchandise for next season. Then Jane organizes a pic-nic for the family and crew.

"We put on a display, and everybody brings food," Jane

said of the gathering at Mitch's house.

The Hales put Christmas on a gift certificate. December 25, Bob and Jane join Mitch in Louisiana and Mississippi for the New Year's fireworks season. "We celebrate Christmas the second week in January," said Jane. "Before we leave, we get the family tree, presents, and decorations ready. When all the boys and their families get back, we do Christmas at the farm. The grandkids used to worry Santa wouldn't know to come late. I'd say, 'It's OK. Santa's on a fireworks schedule too.'"

High Steppers March to Own Drum
Buffalo Gals Drill Team

L ike salt and pepper, the Buffalo Gals spice up a parade with their frisky energy. Twirlers' lariats flare, circle, and bounce. White boots flash. Black skirts swish. The forty-five member drum and bugle corps from Buffalo High School double times in southwest Missouri parades to their own beat.

"I think we're really different," said Stephanie Parish. "We have our own pattern. We have a high-knee lift, toe point, and fast cadence. My mother was in the Buffalo Gals the first year, and they

The Buffalo Gals Drill Team is distinguished by its black and white cowgirl outfit and a quick, two-hundred beat step. (Photo courtesy of Jane Hale)

marched the same way."

The Buffalo Gals trademarks are a small step and quick pace which their founder, Richard King, initiated nearly fifty years ago. While other units swing out in long, smooth strides, the Buffalo Gals march to a two hundred beat minute, marked off in half a shoe-length steps. The distinctive semi-trot bounces the girls down the twelve-block route of an average parade.

The Buffalo Gals costume is as much a part of their tradition as their pace. Despite trends to long skirts and full-sleeved gaucho blouses, the Buffalo Gals always wear fringed, short cowgirl skirts and vests. Their color scheme has always been black and white.

The drill team is part of the high school curriculum, meeting daily to earn one credit hour. Qualifying for the elite group is no picnic. Eighth graders practice six months to master songs and routines before trying out.

"Ninety-eight percent of them score well," said Bryan Elhard, group director. "If they're not going to make it, they get discouraged, or I'll take them aside and talk to them."

"We train them in all the material they are going to need," Bryan said. "We delve into cadences, how to play a bugle, and a lot of fundamentals of music. With some kids, we start from scratch. We try to make the freshmen look pretty close to what a junior and senior look like to spectators."

Everyone begins with a bugle. Those who perform well on the brass instruments stay on to master the soprano, baritone, or bass bugle. Others are assigned to drums or flags. Altogether, the corps includes seventeen drums, sixteen bugles, ten flags, and two twirlers.

Once a girl passes the tryout, the practice begins. She

attends regular school sessions, plus twice weekly practices in the summer. "There is a lot of individual work, aside from rehearsal," Bryan said. "There are untold hours where girls who live close practice together on their own."

The corps' repertoire includes ten songs, which Elhard has adapted for drum and bugle. The drum players learn an additional ten patterns to accompany marching.

All must acquire a unified precision march. "What we aim at is to get all the ranks, file, and diagonals straight. When you get the diagonals, everything else is in," Bryan said. He uses photographs of the group, plus pencil and ruler, to help the girls correct foot positions and spacings.

The group travels from Buffalo, a Dallas County community of 2,300, to ten parades in a season, including Lebanon, Branson, and Springfield Christmas parades. They go to Camdenton's Dogwood Festival, and to Independence, Kansas for a Neewollah (Halloween spelled backwards) Festival where fifty thousand spectators gather.

Closer home, the Buffalo Gals perform at basketball and football games. During the year, they have strutted at Bolivar's Southwest Baptist University basketball games and at the state basketball playoffs in Columbia. The girls like the Southwest Missouri State University Homecoming Parade and Springfield's Christmas parade because they can compete with the five or six other drum and bugle corps located in the area.

"At some time, the corps has won a first in every parade it's ever been in," Bryan said. His file cabinets are cluttered with the gold statues won by the current team. Elsewhere in the school are three trophy cases full of other honors garnered since the organization began in 1956.

Though they could march nearly every weekend, Bryan said it's difficult to juggle the Buffalo Gals appearances with other commitments to cheerleading, basketball, and track.

However, their athletic interests make for better marchers. "Kids are stronger and healthier today than when I started," said Bryan. "I used to carry smelling salts with me. I could count on at least one girl fainting along the route."

Festival Weds Ozark History
to Dogpatch, U.S.A.

Hillbilly Days

With a corncob pipe and a do-si-do, Hillbilly Days at Bennett Spring State Park has all the trappings of an old-time Ozark get-together. Jumping frogs, horseshoe pitching, and fiddle contests are reminders of a bygone era. For Hillbilly Days is part county fair, part box social, and part afternoon picnic in the park.

The three-

Hillbilly Days, perennially the third weekend in June, combines playing dress up for the young ones and hoedown for the fleet of foot. (Photo courtesy of Eric Adams, Lebanon Daily Record.)

day festival was first held in 1974 to commemorate the golden anniversary of the Missouri State Parks System. Since then, the Missouri Division of Parks and Recreation, the Bennett Spring Association, and the Lebanon Chamber of Commerce have wedded the real-life history of area Ozarkers with the fictional high jinks of Dogpatch, U.S.A.

Marryin' Sam couldn't do it better. Park Superintendent Sam Allen estimated that eight thousand guests drop by for Hillbilly Days. The celebration always starts on the second Friday in June. It hooks visitors with a catfish fry and nearly a hundred booths displaying handmade items from "Log Cabin" quilts to rendered soap, homespun wool yarn, and string rugs. Music circles mandolin, classic bluegrass, and country-western twangs. Western square dancers in starched crinolines, gingham dresses, and string neckties follow the directions of veteran callers.

If the promenade-left sets too sedate a pace on Friday, Saturday's events gear up like a country hoedown jig dance. Contests spread through the park like butter on a roasting ear. On the banks above Goodin' Holler, men dressed in buckskin leggings,

Family games from the past are part of the fun during Hillbilly Days at Bennett Spring State Park and Lebanon, Missouri. (Photo courtesy of Eric Adams, Lebanon Daily Record.)

knee-high moccasins, and black powder horns load their flint-lock and Hawken replicas for a primitive weapons shoot. For border state residents who still call it the War Between the States, the appearance of Yankee blue and Johnny Reb gray is a chance to relive history. While their womenfolk watch in long dresses, members of the Civil War Skirmish Association shoot at paper targets in individual competitions.

Meanwhile, the enjoyment of three hundred children is infectious. They hop, scramble, and giggle through sack races, spoon races, and an apple bob. Rummaging through a haystack for hard candy and nickels is the last game before the afternoon's highlight—the greased pig race. Two hapless porkers are generously larded and chased until someone can hold the bacon for sixty seconds.

Teepees and primative weapon competitions add both wood smoke and gunpowder to Hillbilly Days Festival. (Photo courtesy of Patti Whitacre.)

Horseshoe-pitching and pipe-smoking contests offer less rigorous competitions. Gene Glaser of St. Charles set a record, keeping his one-ounce bowl of tobacco lit for sixty-one minutes, twenty-one seconds.

Evening festivities shift to Lebanon, where an estimated ten thousand attend critter races and tobacco-spitting contests. Little Miss and Mister Dogpatch are selected, and Daisy Mae and Li'l Abner look-alikes are chosen. Lebanon resident Effie Cummins is always the one to beat in the hog calling and Mammy Yokum contests. Beyond the wash tub bands, the dunking booth, the car smash, and the roller-skating show, the evening's high moment belongs to the fiddle contest. For every Ozark mountain country native responds to genuine hill music.

The first sound, a long straight resonant note from the fiddlers, electrifies the crowd. Conversation stops; toes tap; hands clap. Young couples break from the crowd to jig. "Your feet just gets to itching if you can't do something with the music," explained one young dancer with taps on her cowboy boots.

Sunday's events return to Bennett Spring for brush arbor worship and an antique car display. The final musket com-

The three-day event features merchandise that is both homespun and hand-done. Craft demonstrations and booths from all over the country fill large tents and spill out onto the park grass. (Photo courtesy of Eric Adams, Lebanon Daily Record.)

petitions fire off after morning services.

For three Hillbilly Days each year, Ozarkers lay aside the natural reserve and quiet dignity central to their character. They paint on freckles, blacken their teeth, and take off their shoes for good times in them thar' hills—real Ozark mountains and otherwise.

Whistlin' Dixie

Civil War Reenactments

L ike ground-level thunder, the gun reports split the tranquility of the fisherman across the spring. When the smoke clears at Bennett Spring State Park's Hillbilly Days Festival, a page of history has come to life. In Civil War uniforms, the men clench the next bullet in their

The Fourth Missouri Infantry Confederate States Army performs reenactments throughout the state.

teeth, pour black powder into the musket barrel, seat the bullet with the ramrod, and fire again.

Unlike their namesakes a century ago, members of the modern day Fifth Regiment of the First Missouri Brigade of the Army of West Tennessee are not shooting at Northerners. They take aim at stationary targets, hoping to win first place trophies in the Civil War Skirmish Association competition.

Duane Hillhouse of Macks Creek and friends stepped into the past after watching a reenactment of the Battle of Lexington on television. "We had been talking about forming a club, something the whole family could enjoy. When we saw that, everything fell into place," Hillhouse said.

Hillhouse contacted the North-South Skirmish Association, which referred them to its sister organization, the Civil War Skirmish Association. The men picked their regiment, researched its history, made a uniform code, took a unit picture, and participated in two official competitions.

Though Missouri remained in the Union during the war between the States, Hillhouse and his friends wanted to take the name of a Confederate unit, preferably the Missouri State Guard where some of their family had served. When they discovered its men disbanded and joined the 3rd and 5th regiments of the 1st Missouri Brigade, they chose the latter. The new 5th became Duane Hillhouse (Macks Creek), David Hillhouse and Bill Porter (Lebanon), George Olson (Ava), Danny Hillhouse (Edwardsville, Ill), Kevin Bowman (Morgan), Marvin Pine (Jefferson City), Bill Moulder (Sunrise Beach), Bob Northcott (Gravois Mill), David Spaulding and Terry Trustley (Eldon).

The history of the Confederate group is as vital a part of their hobby as the wool uniforms their wives make for them, the reproductions of the Civil War weaponry they use, and the minie balls they mold. Names like Price, Shelby, Wilson's Creek and Vicksburg slip easily into their conversations.

"The 1st Missouri Brigade was considered the storm troopers of the Army of West Tennessee," said Duane Hillhouse, possessor of the red sash of regiment commander. "If there was a gap in the line, they were sent to fill it. If there was a place that needed to be taken, they took it. They were the Stonewall Jackson Brigade of the Army of West Tennessee." When the war began, twenty-one hundred men made up the brigade. By the end, its sixty survivors were among the last to surrender.

Hillhouse's 5th Missouri Brigade raises its blue and red flag with its white cross about six times a year in Civil War Skirmish Association competitions and inter-company shoots. The two-day meets are organized into individual and team confrontations. While the women folk watch in long dresses and the children wear miniature versions of their father's chosen side, these Confederate and Union soldiers shoot at bullseyes with muskets, carbines, and pistols. The five-man teams line up in front of six different timed competitions, reminiscent of Civil War shooting.

In the silhouette volley, each team fires on command. After "ready-aim-fire," they have three seconds to shoot at the target, echoing the fire-by-company tactic used to cause casualties and repel an enemy group charge.

Each of the other categories—twelve hanging clay pigeons, twenty mounted clay pigeons, Styrofoam cups, and water-filled balloons are accuracy races with the clock like the real-life need to fire and reload as rapidly as possible. In the 1860s, a man could get off three shots a minute, picking out a new bullet from his pouch, pouring powder, seating the bullet at the bottom of the barrel next to the powder, putting on the cap, and then firing.

The 5th has traditionally finished well in its competitions with all the events except the "stake out." In the past, they have struggled to beat their friendly rivals, the Union's 13th Missouri Infantry. But "Dixie" played loud and long at the Bennett Spring State Park's Hillbilly Days. During this longstanding June festival, the Southern sharpshooters were the first to shoot the particle board stake in two, finishing off the Yankees in six minutes and thirty-eight seconds.

While target shooting is the main concern for the 5th, some members have participated in Civil War reenactments, reliving the Battles of Lexington, Independence, Heritage Village, and Fort Davidson.

Being in a Civil War Skirmish unit is not an inexpensive hobby. Initially members acquire an Enfield or Zouave frontloading musket, costing about two hundred dollars. The bullet and cap pouches, the belt, and shoulder strap run from twenty to sixty dollars, and the wool blend material for the uniform has a forty dollar price tag. After that, buying lead for the eight hundred minie balls the teams use per meet and traveling expenses comprise the major outlays.

It's not so much financial investment as historical involvement that matters to the men who stand at attention during the competition awards ceremonies. "We're proud of the Heritage," said David Hillhouse. With Old Glory and the Stars and Bars billowing full in the breeze, they savor the satisfaction of a challenge met and a legacy remembered—the 5th regiment of First Missouri Infantry of the Army of West Tennessee.

Wade in, Cast Out

Fishing Season Opens

Trout season opens at Bennett Spring State Park as three thousand fishermen and five thousand onlookers stand elbow to elbow along the most important mile and a half of the three thousand acre park. They wait to line the dam's spillway and circle the deep water near the three-arch native rock bridge.

"When the sirens go off, all you hear is the swish of reels," said Sam Allen, Park Superintendent. "It's a festive occasion. It's the opening of spring. There's a lot of camaraderie, a lot of reunions of people who meet once a year."

Star attraction at Bennett Spring, Missouri's most visited state park, is a mile and a half of pristine waters, stocked with rainbow trout.

Waiting for the 6:30 a.m. wade-in on March 1 has its own traditions. All night, fishermen gather in front of the park office and around a dozen bonfires that scatter along the spring bank. Their talk is about trout and new ways to catch it.

Even when the forecast is favorable, nothing's taken for granted about the weather. "You look for bad weather. On March 1, it can rain, snow, or sleet," Allen said. He recalled the 1980 opening day, when temperatures hovered around ten degrees and his staff spent the night shoveling sand and cinders to improve traction on roads and inclines near the spring banks.

"We had thirty-five hundred fishermen and about twice that many onlookers," Allen said. Prudent fishermen make opening day reservations for cabins and hookup campsites months in advance.

The rainbow trout could care less about the weather. Water temperature of the hundred million gallons which flow from "The Eye of the Sacred One" is a constant fifty-six degrees. Conservation Department Hatchery Manager Ron McCullough said nine thousand foot-long trout and two hundred lunkers weighing between two and eight pounds are released for opening day. That's a ratio of 3 1/2 fish per tag in the park. An additional fifteen hundred fish are released in the Niangua River where the spring empties.

The park office and store remain open all night prior to opening day so the crowd can purchase the trout tags. The Dining Lodge prepares for six hundred breakfasts. Once the siren blows, the fishing season for another year has begun.

From Pan to Plate

Country Cookin'

"We're just country cooks here," claimed Anna Belle Simpson, Dining Lodge manager at Bennett Spring State Park. "We cook by taste, texture, and feel. We like our cooks to give their own touch to the menu."

Popularity of house specialities divide almost evenly between Friday evening's fish buffet and breakfast entrees.

After the hard work of catching the rainbow trout is done, Bennett Spring Lodge will cook it for the fisherman's dinner.

First-time tourists, perennial vacationers, and local clientele stoke up on generous portions and down-home cooking the Dining Lodge serves.

Head cook LeRoy Boston supervises the catfish fillet as it's chunked, batter-dipped, and deep-fried. "I know what's in the batter," he said slyly, "but I'm not telling."

The recipe, coupled with a short seven-minute cooking time makes a crust that's crunchy but not hard. The fish is well-done but not greasy. "If it breaks apart good—it's ready," Boston said. "Over cooking makes it greasy."

Though the buffet items include fried chicken, mashed potatoes and gravy, hush puppies, and hot bread, most popular accompaniments to the catfish are corn on the cob, baked beans, and the Lodge's own special potato chip.

"We do something unique to our potatoes," said Mrs. Simpson. "We put them through the dishwasher soap cycle and all." The process, Boston's idea, cleans away the potato jacket's grit.

Foods prepared from scratch—the fish batter, cobbler thickening and buttermilk house dressing—reflect a reluctance to overpower the palate with sugars, oils, or mayonnaise.

The Dining Lodge will cook a fisherman's catch to order and serve it with salad bar, hot bread, and vegetable of the day. About forty sportsmen a month bring their whole, cleaned trout for broiling or frying in the Dining Lodge's iron skillet.

Though well-reputed for its baking powder biscuits and sausage gravy, the Lodge flips out a stellar stack of hot cakes. Cooks add a splash of vanilla and sugar to their basic pancake batter. The light, golden circles hardly require syrup for moistness or sweetening. "It's just in knowing the right batter," Simpson explained.

On Sunday, floaters, fishermen in chest waders, or local residents in church finery opt for the breakfast buffet. The Lodge adds complimentary fruit bar and orange muffins to the scrambled eggs, hash browns, sausage, bacon, biscuits, or toast. "I think people need something special on Sunday," explained Mrs. Simpson. The Bennett Spring Dining Lodge, with its stone walls and cathedral ceiling, provides it.

The Ripple Effect

Charlie Reading's Fly Rods

Charlie Reading is hooked. For three decades he's flicked his line across the currents of Ozark rivers and streams. He's waded the waters of Central America, New Guinea, and Australia. A Renaissance man, he follows the fly on his line more for recreation, art, philosophy, and finance than for the fish.

The object of his intentions is not really the fillet. His devotion springs from the intellectual challenge of a good fighting fish and the pleasures of the location where he finds

Fifty-seven layers create the design on Charlie Reading's own fly rod.

it. "Basically any fish that hasn't been caught on a fly sounds interesting to me," he said. "The more obscure, the more interesting. If a fish has good gaming qualities and is an esthetically pleasing environment, then I'll go there."

His wish list of catches might include the Nile Perch, Atlantic Salmon, or Sea Run Browns. Though the prospects in New Zealand, British Columbia, or the Yucatan might lure him, his favorite fish is not so rare.

"Trout best exemplifies the multiplicity of fly fishing," said Charlie. "It's very selective on what it takes. It's found on top or underneath the surface, in fast or slow water. It's in beautiful settings—mountain lakes, brooks, streams—all over the world. It has vivid, beautiful colors. But fly fishing isn't just the fish. It's being able to make intelligent choices capturing it."

Having netted the moment, Charlie, the philosopher, unfastens the hook. His Fly Shop, located a few miles east of Bennett Spring State Park, sports no mounted trophies of past conquests. The rainbow trout, crowding ledges above the merchandise, are wood-carved models. Not even the tarpon that hangs over the doorway is real. It is a fiberglass replica of the hundred-thirty pound fish he snagged on a fly in the Florida Keys.

"I don't kill fish any more," Charlie explained. "In the first place, I don't want to fool with them. Besides, killing them is just proof to someone else I can fish. It may go back to that idea, fishermen are liars: If you can't show it, you didn't catch it. My own enjoyment of fly fishing is in just doing it. It doesn't mean I don't want results. It just means I enjoy what I'm doing when I'm doing it."

Reading's reputation with the fly unreels past the water.

When Reading the artist touches a fly rod, his work is instantly recognizable. A Reading fly rod catches the essences of fly-fishing: the glint of the sun, the color of water, the flight and fight of the fish. Wrapped in nylon threads, dull graphite deepens to cobalt, shimmers to aquamarine, or ripens to crimson. His cork handles are inset with ring-width wooden bands in dusk's muted pinks. Abalone or pava shell button the handle ends. Fourteen-carat chain loops in channels like golden fishing line. Tiny hooks, smaller than fish scales, circle the grip.

On the rod shaft itself, Charlie creates intricate patterns. Some thinner than needles, fifty-seven layers of feathers form the design on Reading's personal rod.

"I wanted an interesting theme that adds to the enjoyment of the rod," said Charlie of the feather concept he created in 1978. "Feathers and the fly rod fit together like fingers. Feathers go on to the end of the fly line, so I put them on the rod."

Complementing the shaft color, Charlie begins with sapphire, ruby, and emerald feathers to form the iridescent background layer. Obtained from an Ohio friend's exotic birds, the feathers are naturally dropped in molting. He doesn't need many. One neck feather supplies the color for six fly rods. His trademark feather is the Gray Jungle Fowl. Recalling its significance in classic salmon flies, Reading finishes each custom rod with it. Its browns, blacks, and whites form the finger-length design, repeated four times around the rod shaft.

Each Reading rod is built with customer input. "It never looks like somebody just put a feather into epoxy and left it there," said Charlie. Though his art-in-motion customers spread out to Washington and New Zealand, George Bush is the most well-known recipient of a Reading custom rod.

"I was told he liked bonefish and small mouth bass, so I used both a light salt water theme and a heavy fresh water theme. I put in a scrimshawed ivory button depicting a bass. A bonefish is shown in micarta."

Charlie embellished the First Fisherman's rod with African blackwood, water buffalo horn, black-lipped mother-of-pearl, Indian stag, and about a hundred fifty feathers. Reading invested a hundred twenty hours in Bush's rod, about four times more than normal. It was presented in the Oval Office by Trout Unlimited while Bush was President.

Though fully half of Reading's Fly Shop is designated for rod making, his work area is actually just chair size. Spools of thread, epoxy bottles, and blank rods hide his desk. Bookshelves are crammed full; books, magazines, and art prints obliterate the floor.

Charlie the businessman has no interest in his rod work spreading to the other side of Reading's Fly Shop. The west part of Reading's log cabin is jammed with fishing apparel, inflatable pontoons, fly displays, and waders. Factory built rods stack up around the room like cattails rimming a pond. Longtime customers, from Pennsylvania to Kansas, seek out his advice. Casual drop-ins pull off Highway 64 en route to Bennett Spring two miles away. They wade into Charlie's conversations, bantering about techniques, their afternoon intentions, and stories about the big one that got away.

Once fishing season gears up, Charlie sticks close to home. The trip to the Falkland Islands waits until fall. Making fly rods is relegated to after supper hours. Once opened, Bennett Spring will host a hundred eighty thousand fishing aficionados during its March to October season. To further promote the area and the sport, Charlie helps organize the Bennett Spring Fly Fishing Conclave. Held the first weekend in May, experts with national reputations give lessons and workshops for both the inexperienced and the accomplished.

"Bennett Spring is probably one of the finest spring creeks in the world," said Charlie, who has spent a dozen years at his present location just east of the park entrance. "It does a lot of good. Many people feel connected to this place because they learned to fly fish here."

If any man could put his life into one net, Charlie Reading can do it. Talking sport, he's soon philosophizing. The philosophizing fishtails into art. Art spawns business. Talking about it, designing, or casting it, nothing makes a ripple around Charlie Reading like fly fishing.

Charlie Reading discusses trout catching techniques with customers at Reading's Fly Shop under a replica of the tarpon he caught in Florida.

Sibling Revelry

Carolyn Gray Thornton and Ellen Gray Massey

Carolyn Gray Thornton and Ellen Gray Massey's sister act has thrived seven decades, from climbing trees to publishing books. Thornton's *A Funny Thing Happened on the Road to Senility: I Discovered the Joy of Middle Age Plus* and Massey's *Merryman's*

In 1938, Carolyn Gray (left) was a substitute centerfielder, while older sister, Ellen "was the star third baseman of the neighborhood team." (Photo courtesy of Ellen Gray Massey)

Ellen Gray Massey

Crossing hit the bookshelves at the same time. Their joy was a shared success.

Thornton uses the bathroom mirror and senior citizen discounts for her wry observations of active living after fifty. Massey, the novelist, focuses on the Ozarks she loves.

These sisters share a friendship thicker than blood. The youngest of eight siblings, the sisters lived in Washington, D.C. where their father lobbied for a farmer's organization and spent summers in Nevada. They played baseball, planned square dances, and roomed in college together. Later, each with children and spouses, they shared cross-country vacations and float trips.

"Carolyn would take risks I wouldn't," admitted Ellen. "She meets strangers more easily than I do. She is fun to be around."

"Ellen would invent plays to act out with our paper dolls," Thornton said of the days when they grinned in tandem from family photos. "She'd start a project, and I'd tag along as the gofer. I admire her ability to follow through with her dreams. My book was her dream for me."

A Funny Thing Happened on the Road to Senility developed from Massey's big-sister bossing. Its hundred essays originate from Thornton's column, "Middle Age Plus," weekly musings

for those with thinning eye-
brows, thickening waist-
lines, and hair sprouting
where it shouldn't.

"Let's make a pact
together," she said. "I will
not look at the skin on your
neck if you will not look at
mine."

She recalls leg makeup
and cars with running
boards, but her backward
vision is clear-eyed.
Thornton prefers the pre-
sent to the days with ice-

Carolyn Gray Thornton

boxes, wringer washers, and air-raid drills.

"There's nothing we can do about the aging process,"
she said. "I find humor in it and just keep on going. I get my
ideas on the riding lawn mower," she said.

Thornton's journalistic career developed in 1993. Ellen
invited her sister to a writer's critique group where Thornton
read an essay about her first great grandchild. Inspired by its
reception, Thornton approached the *N.E.W. Vernon County
Record* about writing a column on the pluses of the senior
years. When Thornton accumulated several dozen columns,
Ellen suggested they compile a book.

"I thought they should go beyond the readership of her
newspaper," said Ellen. "Carolyn was more modest about
their appeal and was involved in other things."

Thornton's husband, Lester, had officially retired in
1988 from the ministry, and they had returned to their farm
next to "The Wayside." He soon took interim and associate

pastorates and continued overseeing the Gray family's acreage. Thornton directed The Neighbors, Nevada's adult day care program, helped care for her great grandchild and her oldest sister, taught Sunday School class with her husband, and participated in professional women's organizations. "That was before I retired one of my many times," said Carolyn, who then became a VISTA volunteer in Habitat for Humanity.

Still, Massey persisted—for four years. "She just would not leave me alone until I did something," said Carolyn. When she finally relented, the sisters organized the manuscript on Ellen's living room floor. In 1999, Ellen took their collaboration to an Alabama writers' conference and approached Dallas publisher, Jim Harris. *A Funny Thing Happened on the Road to Senility* resulted.

Ellen's ninth novel, *Merryman's Crossing*, was coincidentally published at the same time. Her novels are set in the Ozarks, from Nevada and Columbia, south to Lebanon. Massey has been preserving the region's customs since her tenure as creator/advisor of *Bittersweet* magazine. Lebanon high school students from 1973 to 1983 published the quarterly. Ellen edited two *Bittersweet* anthologies, three other novels, and Carolyn's book. Currently she conducts Ozark studies for Drury College Graduate Education program and for Elderhostel groups at the YMCA of the Ozarks at Potosi.

Ellen's own writing ambitions found print a decade ago, after she retired from public school teaching. Critiqued and advised by Carolyn, she's authored the award-winning biography of Ozark poet, Mary Elizabeth Mahnkey, historical novels, and family-reading Avalon books.

"My books usually include a river and a cave," said

Ellen. "Those geographical aspects of the Ozarks fascinate me. They help form the character of the people here."

Ellen knows *Crossing's* river as the Osage Fork of the Gasconade in Laclede County. Ellen and her husband, Lane, pastured three hundred ten acres there. Her book's fictional bridge is modeled on the Davis Mill Bridge. After her husband's death, Ellen maintained the farm while teaching in Hartville for three years. On the fifty-mile round trip, she often crossed flooded low water bridges—a situation central to the book's plot.

"I used to say my car was half boat," she recalled. "I've done all these things, so it's easy to write about them."

Ellen used Mary Elizabeth Mahnkey's country store at Oasis for *Crossing's* country store, the heroine's inheritance from her grandparents. Ellen's fictional cave is based on a long-undiscovered cave a student in her evening class accidentally found.

"In the Ozarks, people work hard to make a living from the land. It doesn't give easily. Yet, everything's here if you're willing to work for it—both physically and mentally," said Ellen. "The book shows the spirit of the people who wouldn't let their traditions go."

Ellen's *Borderland Homecoming*, another Avalon book, was published February 2000. A month later, her two-act play, *A Life I Can See*, was produced at Lebanon's Cowan Civic Center. No less active, Carolyn presides over the 11,700 members of the Missouri West conference of United Methodist Women, continues her column, and lawn work.

The
Lights of
LEBANON

Ozark Soul

Rodney Dangerfield in Overalls

In the past, when I'd introduce myself as Ozarks
grounded, I'd get the
Rodney Dangerfield shuffle.
People shifted their feet and
moved the conversation elsewhere. Their eyes glazed
over; they'd glance at their
watch or edge toward the buffet table. Perhaps they
sneaked a peek to see if I had
on shoes, although no one ever
asked what nail I kept my
overalls on.

*Mothers, movie stars and preschoolers
hook the suspenders and twist those durn
side buttons through the holes.*

But the Plateau is not so much a geographic orphan as a long-lost relative. If Easterners think it's too far west to be East, and Westerners think it is too far east to be embraced as the West, perhaps a family reunion is in order. The creativity and character of the Ozarks reaches into law, medicine, food, fashion, history, art, and literature in every part of the country.

The boundary dispute between Alaska and Canada was settled by a Missourian. The nation's first speed limit—nine miles an hour—began here. The inventor of the stomach pump, the wire suspension splint, depth charges, and developer of quinine have roots in the Show-Me state.

Want a Dairy Queen on a hot day? The St. Louis 1904's World Fair inaugurated the first ice cream cone, the hot dog, and iced tea. Want something stronger? Not moonshine, but just up the street from my house, Independent Stave Company constructs the white oak barrels that flavor the scotch, whiskey, and California wines enjoyed throughout the world.

Authors from the Ozarks fill university and library shelves. Missouri claims poets T.S. Elliot, Ezra Pound, Eugene Field, and Sara Teasdale. Sam Clemens is required reading in any American literature course. A couple of miles from Mansfield's town square, a simple farm woman named Laura Ingalls Wilder wrote her gentle pioneer stories. Harold Bell Wright, now a name dusty with the past, was a *New York Times* best-selling author, a millionaire during hard times.

In September, millions of five-year-olds will trudge off to school because the first kindergarten was organized in Missouri. When the bell rings for lunchtime, and they unwrap that classic peanut butter and jelly sandwich, they should thank George Washington Carver.

Gilt-framed landscapes and murals from Missouri artists, George Caleb Bingham and Thomas Hart Benton, are museum masterpieces. If their themes are too formal or political for family room decoration, there's always a bath towel or a clock or a telephone or a shower curtain or wallpaper in the likeness of those cartoon mice, creations of Missouri-born, Walt Disney.

In war, Ozark soldiers fought bravely. Missouri's role in the Civil War is well documented. Sixty percent of Missouri's eligible men fought in the War Between the States, the highest percentage of any state in the Union. The Mexican War took a turn in our direction because 800 Missouri volunteers overwhelmed 4,000 Mexican troops. John Pershing led in the first World War, and Omar Bradley served with five stars in the second. Harry Truman decided "The Buck Stops Here" and dropped the atomic bomb, oversaw the Marshall Plan, Berlin Airlift, and NATO during his administration.

That silver loop in St. Louis, now the nation's tallest monument, shines there for a reason. Adventurers pushed their boats into the mighty Mississippi and Missouri Rivers to find the West. Those who didn't have a paddle likely jostled across The Plains in a Murphy wagon. A little known St. Louisan named Joseph Murphy made the first wagon to reach the Continental Divide—and 200,000 more during his career. Their wheels, seven feet tall and eight inches wide, cut trails that can still be seen. Charles Russell, one of the West's great artists, was born in St. Louis. Jim Bridger, most famous mountain man of them all, started out there too. Jesse James, Belle Starr, Calamity Jane, "Wild Bill" Hickock all jangled their spurs across the state.

In more recent times, Emmett Kelley's "Sad Willie," the circus clown, made us happy; Scott Joplin's music made us smile; and Brad Pitt still makes us sigh.

My small town of Lebanon, just off Interstate 44, has produced a Director of the U.S. Treasury, a federal judge, and a Pulitzer Prize winner. Harold Bell Wright wrote *Shepherd of the Hills* here. Lebanon is the aluminum boat manufacturing capital of the world. And that's just my hometown. I've lived in Missouri two decades and am still discovering its historical wealth. One wonderful source is *Across Our Wide Missouri*, three volumes of essays by Bob Priddy, radio journalist from Jefferson City. The rich heritage of the Arkansas and Oklahoma Ozarks fill a lifetime of reading.

Now, understandably our cornpone image has been somewhat self inflicted. After all, when outsiders asked where the hillbillies were, we dressed up in overalls and pretended to be them.

Still, overalls are everywhere these days. Long overalls, short overalls, overall jumpers, denim overalls, khaki overalls, and plaid overalls cover toddlers and teenagers. Mothers and movie stars hook up the suspenders and twist those durn side buttons through the holes. Of course, the brands have changed. Besides Big Smith and Oshgosh labels, I see fashionable New York names and initials sewn on the front pocket. Their price tag has more digits. Come to think of it, this may be a good sign. Maybe the rest of the country is finally catching up.

Love's Curtain Call
Our Town Reprised

If love could have a curtain call, the cast of *Our Town* earned it. As carefree teenagers in 1978, they first performed Thornton Wilder's play. Two decades later, now seasoned adults, they reprised their roles on the same stage. Only this time, the most important actor wasn't there.

Cheri Jo Davis died in a car accident one month into her senior year. The thirty-three members of the original troupe returned to their Ozark hometown to honor their sweet-faced friend and reestablish a performing arts scholarship in her name.

Cast members from seven states and sixteen cities returned to honor their classmate, Cheri Jo Davis, who died in a car accident in 1979. (Photo courtesy of Charlotte Davis)

The reunion performance began with Gary Newton,

their male lead in the Pulitzer Prize drama. Now a California screenwriter, Newton discovered the family's memorial for Jo had depleted.

"It seemed a shame it wasn't continuing," he said. "I thought we should do something about it."

Half a continent and two decades from drama class in Lebanon, Missouri, Newton struggled locating the old gang. Finally, the Davis family, who still had newspaper clippings of 1978 production and Jo's costumes, sent him a program listing the participants. Over fourteen months, Newton tracked them through seven states and sixteen cities. Classmates willingly committed to the project, leaving responsibilities as judge, policeman, teacher, oncologist, weatherman, homemaker, and bank president for a three-act performance from the past.

Small wonder. Jo Davis was full of life, busy laughing and singing country music. She taught Sunday School, used lunch money to buy friends presents, and paid attention to quiet acquaintances she passed at school.

When asked about performing again in the play, Alan Scott, a pediatrician, said, "First, I thought, that would be fun. Then, we can't pull anything off that big. When I realized it was for Jo, it was a given. As first graders, we sat together on a little red bench in Sunday School. She was a lifelong friend."

Newton sent the cast newsletters, reconnecting those who'd lost touch and updating the project's progress. He contacted an Atlanta documentary crew to film the experience from get-acquainted party to final performance.

Still, he hadn't solved who would play Jo's character, ten-year-old Rebecca Webb or how the project would be

In 1978 Gary Newton and Caroline Van Stavern play "George" and "Emily" who marry in Our Town. *(Photo courtesy of Gary Newton)*

financed. Newton again turned to the Davis family and found Jo's niece, ten-year-old Joanna Bellis busily tending her Hereford calves and practicing gymnastics.

"Joanna is my sister's namesake," said her mother, Carla Bellis. "The part fitted her spontaneity. She loves performing at church. She doesn't get nervous and memorizes easily."

"I practiced almost every day," said Joanna, who used her aunt's old play book. "I tried giving expression to my lines."

Locally owned Central Bank stepped from the wings to underwrite all expenses. "*Our Town* is about hometown roots and life's stages. It fit our mission perfectly," explained Craig Curry, its president and Newton's classmate. "Then mistakenly, I said, 'If there's anything else I can do...' Gary gave me the undertaker's role."

The community of 10,000 embraced the project. Businesses donated material to darken the stage, snacks for the marathon rehearsal schedule, and lodging for the film crew. Restaurant marquees welcomed cast alumni. The Davises' church organized a Sunday potluck dinner where the high school choir volunteered to perform "In My Room," sung at Jo's funeral. Though Lebanon's football games or Christmas parades usually pull more crowds than do

Two decades after their first performance of Our Town, cast members rehearse their roles in a fund-raising performance for their classmate. Jo's niece, Joanna Bellis, took her part as Rebecca Webb. (Photo courtesy of Goodwin Photography)

theatrical events, *Our Town's* weekend performances sold out before the doors opened. A Saturday afternoon matinee accommodated overflow requests.

Anne Dryden, their drama teacher, returned to direct. With only three days before performance, the group polished their lines, learned stage directions, and sorted through memories during rehearsals.

"We were a play within a play, our own *Our Town*," observed Dryden of her former students. "Everybody brought back their own life experiences. They were thirty-five-year-olds acting like seventeen-year-olds playing forty-five-year-olds."

"When we were younger, we were hooting and hollering all during rehearsal," said Scott. "Twenty years later, there wasn't a dry eye in the group."

Beyond innocence, they had dealt with birth, death, marriage, and career decisions much as the Gibbs and Webb families do in Wilder's classic. Sequestered between the present and the past, the cast met Wilder's message center stage.

"What touched me was when Emily left the cemetery to relive her twelfth birthday," said Don Massey, now a wholesaler liaison in St. Louis. "She asks, 'Do human beings ever realize life while they live it every, every minute?' That hit me hard. Then I tried to make the most of this experience, to really look at everyone and enjoy the moment."

After each performance, both cast and audience were reluctant to bring the curtain down on the experience. Former teachers, classmates, friends climbed on stage, hugging and laughing with the actors, with Jo's parents, and with her sisters' families.

Sunday, the cast gathered at the White Oak Pond Cumberland Presbyterian Church. Newton's tribute recalled the seventeen-year-old who had touched all their lives. He

In 1999, Gary Newton and Caroline Van Stavern reprise their roles as "George" and "Emily." (Photo courtesy of Goodwin Photography)

thanked the community for raising over $15,000 for Jo's performing arts scholarship.

Was it coincidence that the congregational song, "I'll Fly Away," was Jo's favorite and that the offertory, "Blest Be the Tie That Binds," was in *Our Town*?

"We had planned the music earlier," the director said. "I didn't realize its significance until I saw the play."

Surrounded by warm spring winds and fresh green fescue fields, the country church was a fitting place to honor the past and appreciate the future. "This play reunion made us realize the impact we have on others' lives," said Scott. "So much time has gone by. My kids are growing up. I've already missed out on a lot. Next time Alex wants me to play, and the grass needs mowing, I'm going to shoot baskets."

The legacy of Jo Davis continues on. In her name, the cast of *Our Town* returned a scholarship to their childhood's community. In her name, they took away far more—an awareness for life's every moment and the desire to savor it.

What better encore to love?

Knee-High Fun at the Ballpark

Little League

Their red, green, and yellow hats bob down the street like tethered balloons. For this show these Little League youngsters put on their uniforms, gather around a team sign, and parade past bystanders. They are ready for summer.

The 700 Little League children who halt traffic on Saturday morning are part of a larger network of Lebanon baseball lovers, not unlike would-be little leaguers elsewhere in the Ozarks and the nation.

Participants range from awkward kindergartners who grope for balls trickling between their legs to graceful athletes who hit the ball in high arcs over center field fences.

Participants range from awkward kindergartners who grope for balls trickling between their legs to graceful athletes who hit the ball in high arcs over center field fences. "There is a team for anyone who wants to play, from six years old to sixty," said Charlie Walker, Lebanon Little League president.

Including Little League, 108 teams totaling 2,000 players fill rosters for the city's nine fields. Players find spots in the Little Leagues, three divisions of Babe Ruth League, girls' primary and intermediate fast pitch, women's slow pitch, men's slow pitch industrial and church teams.

For some families, with members on more than one team, the April to July season is a way of life. Nine months pregnant, Liz Whitt chauffeured her eight-year old to Little League Midget practice on Monday, checked in with her Springfield obstetrician on Tuesday, drove her six-year-old to Tee-ball on Wednesday, and in her spare time watched her husband, Jim, play four nights a week in church and industrial games.

"I knew it was going to be this way before I got married," she said of her perennial bleacher vigils. "But I might as well be here watching than sitting at home waiting for something to happen."

Some parents use a car pool or drop kids off to create time for running errands during twice-weekly practices. However, on game nights, the whole family—grandparents to newborns—take seats in bleachers to cheer.

Between innings, they may converse about their hectic schedules or the fast-food supper they'll pick up or the end-of-season tournaments. But talk is just miscellaneous filler until their child touches bat or ball.

Then the conversation dies. Backs straighten. Legs uncross. Tongues loosen and the chatter gets personal: "Good try." "What a swing." "Make him pitch to you, son."

If the coach is busy with batting order substitutions, some fathers take the opportunity for a few private instructions through the backstop or dugout fence. Youngsters react either with stoicism or grateful grins toward that voice they know so well. Said one boy after losing a close call at first, "My mom—she always claps."

On the field, Tee-ball beginners seem befuddled. There is so much to remember: *Swing the bat; don't throw it. Hit the ball. Run straight, even if someone is going to tag you out. Don't drop the ball behind you or throw it into the dirt. Don't lose your brother's glove.* Their kindergarten and first-grade attention spans take refuge in more familiar jostling with friends or drawing figures in the dirt.

By age seven, kids shed oversized shirts and hats for uniforms. They acquire a batting glove, a wad of bubble gum, and the ability to catch back handed. They discriminate between pitched balls and strikes. The easy grace of an emerging athlete flashes in the swing of the bat or the sweep to tag a runner.

Further up the Little League ladder, Majors and Minors players polish their skills. The pitcher works from a mound and stands ten feet back from the Midget mark.

Babe Ruth athletes, ages thirteen to eighteen, split into three divisions and are chosen in a point drafting system. Pitchers throw from the stretch; batters can bunt, lead off base, and run ninety-foot baselines. At the end of the season, they hope to be named to one of fourteen for all-star tournament play.

In the squeeze play between players and parents is the coach. Passion for the sport lured Lloyd Tabor into the hot spot ten years ago. Beginning a year before his son was born, he has worked with the ten- to twelve-year-olds in the Minors system.

"You can start with a boy who has no confidence, and if you have patience, you can build him up to be a pretty good little player," Tabor said.

J.L. Kinnett played Little League himself and helped coach when he was thirteen. Two decades later, he managed two teams, the Midget Pirates and Babe Ruth Angels. "You can't do it for one and not for the other," he explained of his two sons.

Kinnett varies his approach at the two age levels. With the older boys, capable of basic baseball maneuvers, he coaches by telling. For the seven to nine year olds who hug his neck if they win or think the world ends if they strike out, Kinnett exercises patience and demonstrations. "You have to show them how to hit and how to throw," he said. When they lose, Kinnett said, "I just tell them, 'This is part of growing up.' I say 'Let's go on to the next game and win that one.' Most of the time if I can get the little fellows to smile, chances are they will."

Fancy Dancin'

Les Roderick

C logging just isn't what it used to be, and Les Roderick is one of the reasons why. Long ago, the four-time National Dance America Clogging Champion left the

traditional fringed shirts and barn-dance image for a high-energy interpretation of the original Dutch treat. The Lebanon teenager's favorite dance combines country hoedown, Irish step dancing, Dutch clogging, jazz, and Canadian double tapping. Stainless steel plates on each shoe click off eight sounds to each beat, eight beats in

Les Roderick combines jazz, modern, and clogging steps for Dance America competitions. His trademark hand movements, unusual in clogging, end his performances.

each thirty-nine mea-
sures of his two and a
half-minute routine.

Roderick's size
twelve shoes are
hardly ever on the
floor. The six foot,
two inch sophomore
is mostly airborne,
the consequence of
jumps, stomps, kicks,
hops, and double tap
slaps. Executing 2500
steps in 150 seconds
leaves even Roderick,
an eight hundred
meter and 5K cross-
country runner,
breathing hard.

Les Roderick holds the double-plated clogging shoe which gives him 2500 sounds in a scant 150 seconds.

The fifteen-year-old has been clogging nearly a decade. "When I was about five, I told Mom 'I'm going to be a clogging teacher when I grow up.'" said Roderick. "Some people have their basketball. For me, clogging is just the thing to do."

Disdaining tap lessons with a room full of girls in his mother's School of Performing Arts, Roderick mastered skills like "the ankle breaker" or "karate turn" early on. Though both his mother and his sister teach dance, Roderick travels three times a month to Aurora for lessons at Brad Boettler's Clog-O-Mania and team practice with others in Boettler's "Touch of Class" clogging team. Roderick choreographs his own solo work.

"His solo is definitely a hybrid," said Boettler. "He has clogging, modern dance, and jazz. He has a lot of footwork. He's got height and mass. He's able to get a lot of power in the footwork.

"Every clogger knows how hard the Canadian Double-double is to perform. I do them at the end of the two and a half-minute routine," said Roderick. "At state competition, I added hand movements and a yell. When I finished, the crowd was silent for about three counts and then went wild."

Roderick starts with pop, rap, or dance songs like "Runaway" or "Pump Up the Volume." His costumes can be either a flashy silver space suit or baggy street clothes. Year 2000's routine, danced to "Canned Heat" by Jamiroquai, required sequined black. "Whenever you sing, you have to understand what the song means. When I clog, I break down everything in it, too. When I'm on stage, I am the character."

To join the 1800 dancers who competed at the Nationals in Orlando, Roderick must finish first or second in a regional competition in Oklahoma or Missouri. Appearing there requires that his videotaped routine pass preliminary judging—a disappointment a younger Roderick experienced the first time he applied in 1995. He doesn't have that trouble any more.

"A lot of people do good moves, but he is a performer, a real crowd pleaser," said his mother, Dorita. "He's been around dancing, modeling and competitions since he was three. It's just part of him."

Three judges evaluate his individual style, audience appeal, and accurate execution of standard clogging steps.

"You just can't get out there and stomp your feet and call it clogging," said Roderick.

Stage presence might be an inherited talent. His sister, Denette capped a long pageant career as Miss Missouri in the Miss USA Pageant 2000. "I'm her number one fan," Roderick said. "When I'm with her, I meet other beauty pageant contestants, and there's nothing wrong with that. I tell her, 'Hey, I think she's cute. Can you introduce me?'"

Besides competing in Phoenix, Las Vegas, Nashville, Tulsa, Kansas City, St. Louis, and Orlando, Roderick is active in school and community theater productions and modeling. But he is not yet old enough to cash in on his abilities—either making dancing a job or developing his own variation of the clogging shoe. "I'd hollow out the first plate. That would make a deeper sound," he said.

Conditioning for performance is a year long project. "It gets long and grueling," says Roderick. "You have to build your endurance and strength up by doing it every single day."

The New "King" of AM Radio
Jim Bohannon

J im Bohannon is good company. With a smile as wide as the Missouri and a laugh as deep, he is witty, thoughtful, and informed. Just the kind of host you'd like to visit with after dinner, except conversation with the Mutual Broadcasting star

"*I'm a paid mouth,*" *says Jim Bohannon, who hoped to impress the girls in downtown Lebanon and now reaches across the United States. (Photo courtesy of Westwood One)*

goes way beyond coffee on the couch. His living room is a Washington, D.C. sound booth. His guests include two million listeners and the people of *TV Guide, Newsweek, and Sports Illustrated.*The forty-year veteran of talk radio and his console full of callers discourse nightly with celebrities like Jimmy Carter, Mary Higgins Clark, Carol Channing, Pat Buchanan, Jerry

Falwell, and Mohammad Ali. An animal psychic, female boxer, or throneless princess have also dropped by to chat. From 9 p.m. to 12 p.m. Central Standard Time, they dialogue about current events, legislation, scientific breakthroughs, death, or taxes, with a little hero worship thrown in.

"I'm a paid mouth," Bohannon is fond of exclaiming. The gift of glib notwithstanding, there's more to Bohannon than teeth. His several thousand broadcasts and a couple of decades in radio's premier time slot duets to the twin voices defining "The Jim Bohannon Show."

"A program doesn't have to teach an audience," said the master of AM Radio. "I'd like to think my show is both entertaining and enlightening."

Several turns back on the rewind reel, Bohannon's abilities to amuse and analyze developed in his hometown of Lebanon. His "Leave It to Beaver" childhood scampered through the high spirits of "The Red Skelton Show," Boy Scouts, and rivalry with his best friend for first chair trombone. Though memorable for his skin-dyed performance of "Flying Purple People Eater" at his Prom, Bohannon's high school career also introduced him to the wonders of talk and the microphone.

"I was taken by it," Bohannon said of beginning speech class, "and later by interscholastic speech and debate." He picked up the rudiments of verbal dueling, filling briefcases full of news magazines and index-card defenses for debate tournaments. A meager social life for the self-described class nerd sent Bohannon to KLWT radio for an after-school job. Broadcasting on the smallest station in the state, his voice traveled at least downtown where he hoped to impress girls.

Attracting listeners is no longer a problem. Callers from the Virgin Islands to Maine to Texas dial up to visit. His four-hundred affiliate stations crisscross a good chunk of the Western Hemisphere. Every commercial spot is sold, and sponsors want more.

"Most of the things I have today are pure serendipity," said Bohannon. "I'm one of the more fortunate people I've met. Much has been through just dumb luck." At Southwest Missouri State University, he worked part-time at KICK and KWTO. After a tour in Vietnam, Bohannon was transferred to the nation's capitol where he picked up announcing duties at easy-listening radio stations. During a three-year stint as WCFL morning anchor and CNN news reporter in Chicago, a wrench in a rocket launched him into the airwaves he talks on today.

"The space correspondent at Westwood One usually filled in for Larry King, but he was stuck in Cape Canaveral when the lift-off was delayed," recalled Bohannon. "If I could find the mechanic responsible, I swear I'd buy him dinner."

King remembered a technician's oft-repeated praise of Bohannon and asked him to substitute. Filling in for the talk-show legend led to an eleven-year tenure as number one number two. When King left in 1993, Bohannon slid into the late-night time slot full time.

Bohannon's broadcasts air Sunday through Friday in three sixty-minute segments: one-on-one interviews, guest-caller dialog, and listener call-ins.

"I'll talk about anything," he said. Well, not quite. He leaves political harangues for Limbaugh and Ollie North. Bruce Williams and Dr. Laura Schlessinger can have financial and relationship advice. And he refuses to go below the belt for a laugh. "Howard Stern gives some people what they want," Bohannon said, "And he's very good at it. But I simply will not roll around in the muck."

Bohannon, the reporter, turns his guests instead toward such murky issues as campaign finance reform or Hong Kong's return to China. He contacted journalists at the Oklahoma City bombing trial for updates. With an ear toward the volunteerism summit, Bohannon phoned SMSU president John Kaiser about university efforts. On National Freedom of Information Day, (a commemoration Bohannon himself initiated), he questioned *Lebanon Daily Record* publisher Dalton Wright about the future of community newspapers.

"An expert properly chosen gives us all a chance to learn," he explained. "I hope my program makes a contribution to the national dialogue."

If the essence of a talk show host is opinions, Bohannon deserves his top-ten rating. As a "moderate militant," he stands right on defense issues and left with social issues. He worries that policy makers no longer represent the sensible center. "I'm not a raving super patriot," he said, "but I really do love my country, and I am bothered when it seems under assault." Calling the federal shortfall "a bill to the unborn," he supports a Constitutional amendment to balance the budget. Those responsible for the murder of JonBenet Ramsey should "fry, fry very slowly." From his own 1990 keynote address at the Vietnam Memorial, Bohannon lectured Robert McNamara, former Secretary of Defense on air: "Any war worth fighting is worth winning. If it's not worth winning, it's not worth fighting."

Ever mindful of the smile dial, Bohannon also books Reba McIntire, George Carlin, Lucy Arnaz, or the cast of the musical, *Chicago*. But much of the fun depends on Bohannon chewing the fat during open phone lines. He tells his audience, "We can talk about anything we please." Forewarned with only the caller's city and state, he flips the "on" switch for caller choice—women in the military, gun control, or the day's headlines. But the pompous, the ridiculous, or illogical had best beware. They are swiftly and efficiently filleted by his rapier rhetoric.

Everyone feels the point of Bohannon's sense of humor, irony, or justice. He once asked Tom Wopat, the dark-haired Duke of Hazzard, "Couldn't you guys afford a car with doors?"

"Why do they change the needles between executions?" Bohannon mused. "Do they think the condemned will catch something?"

To Mark Fuhrman from O.J. Simpson's trial, "Why should we believe anything you say?"

"I hope my style reflects the type of show I do, with its variety of themes and guests, subjects and seriousness," Bohannon explained. "I don't know if that makes me a chameleon, but I hope it makes me versatile."

Listener response to Bohannon's style spools from adoration to contempt. A Kansas City woman gushed, "Jim, are you married? You've kept me up many nights." Yet, a militia survivalist once threatened to string him up.

"I told him, 'Bring plenty of rope,'" recalled Bohannon. "I couldn't believe the audience support I got after that call."

Most of Bohannon's faithful tune-in from upper income, middle-age strata, like the Dallas public relations consultant who commented, "Listeners want somebody to make sense and ask the insightful question they would ask. He doesn't let anyone get away with a whole lot."

After the broadcast, Bohannon works through the night, preparing "America in the Morning," his a.m. newscast. Retreating to the office which houses his broadcasting awards, second-place trophy as funniest celebrity in Washington, and souvenirs from KLWT, he prepares questions for future interviews. And he polishes the Bohannon trademark prose.

"They're probably the most fun thing I do," he said of the limericks and rhymes that mark his news magazine's introductions. "I write down eight to ten puns and incorporate the lead around them."

Living between the increments of the second hand, Bohannon can use a 70-second break to get coffee for his guests or run off copies at the Xerox machine. Somewhere in a work day turned inside out, he's written *Keeping My Night Job*, which chronicles his assignments at the Moscow summit, France's Bastille Day, Inaugural Parades and vintage Bohannon anecdotes. On weekends he speaks to dinner groups, emcees the National Radio Hall of Fame Awards, or records promos. "Without them," he said of his loyal affiliates, "I'd be the world's largest intercom."

High on the list of great interviews was the one with *Garfield's* Jim Davis. At the low end, there's the interview with a Hawaiian nationalist who tried bullying him for control of the show.

The truth is that Jim Bohannon will never relinquish the microphone. There's too many people yet to talk with. "I'd love to interview Johnny Carson," said Bohannon. "He's one of the great minds ever to sit in front of microphone. He would be a lot of fun. I'd like to have interviewed Boris Yeltsin." Bohannon would ask Bill Cosby, "Did you miss an opportunity by not using racial humor," and query Hillary Clinton with, "Are you as tough as they say you are?"

Despite the celebrities he talks to, Missouri's long-distance son remains steadfastly connected to his hometown.

"I'm very proud of my roots," he said. He regularly emcees the Lebanon Area Foundation concerts and his class of '62 reunions. Visiting his mother, Dorothy, he verbally cruises

Commercial Street for classmates who recall when wearing belts in pant loops was the biggest issue for small-town teens.

Hard-news journalist, humorist, political commentator and connoisseur of new books, Jim Bohannon may be the consummate talk-show host. When misunderstandings and the doldrums menace late-night listeners, like monsters just outside the door, the most important thing Jim Bohannon may ever say is, "We'll be right back."

Going Against the Grain

Barry McKenzie

Barry McKenzie is a man content. His days center around a small-bladed knife and a piece of bass wood. Cutting into its soft surface, he embellishes candlesticks, jewelry and tissue boxes, birdhouses, breadboards, walking sticks, shelves, and mantels. His geometric designs, 1/16th of an inch deep, are filigrees in wood.

"Chip carving changed my life," he admitted. "I had high blood pressure, headaches,

Barry McKenzie knew he was a chip carver when he had completely filled a film cannister with finger-nail-sized wood chips. (Photos by Steve J.P. Laing, Springfield (Mo.) News-Leader.)

stomach problems, and high cholesterol. I had a terrible attitude. Now I'm very complacent."

McKenzie walked away from a twenty-year career, constructing nuclear reactors. With Barbara, his wife, McKenzie fled a fast-lane Chicago lifestyle to develop a hobby into a full time enterprise.

"My boss thought I was nuts. I told him 'I quit. I'm going to teach chip carving. I'm going to start a school, and I'm going to wood carving shows.'"

McKenzie discovered his passion by accident. When he enrolled in a wood-carving course ten years ago, he was just looking for diversion from a job he hated. He thought whittling mallards would do it.

"My instructor told me, 'We don't do ducks here. This is a chip carving class,'" recalled McKenzie. Two hours later, he was hooked on the little-known craft.

Chip carving requires only a soft wood surface, one knife, and patience. Three converging cuts free a chip, as big as a grain of rice, from butternut, poplar, or bass wood. The triple stabs, repeated over and over, create the pattern. McKenzie practiced eighteen months before he felt his skills were honed. "I showed Barbara every time I made a perfect chip. I told her when I'd filled a film canister with perfect chips, I'd call myself a chip carver."

While McKenzie carved toward expertise, the couple planned to relocate. Missouri was centrally located to carving exhibits, and they liked the area's drinking water. Nestled in a grove of trees, the cedar and oak cottage they found on Highway 66 was ideal for their world of wood.

"I want to make Lebanon the center for chip carving," he said. His strategy is three-ringed. He writes a quarterly newslet-

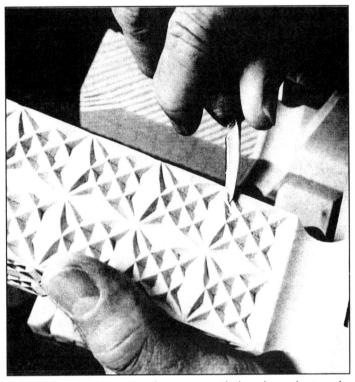

Barry McKenzie's chip carving designs start with three diagonal cuts and a flick of the wrist.

ter, sharing ideas and patterns with other chip carvers who have discovered him. He holds beginning classes at his store, The Craft Barn. Once a month, he goes out-of-state—to Oregon, Texas, Oklahoma, West Virginia—to conduct workshops.

"I introduce the fundamentals in two days. I'll show people how to do it. Then, they have to teach themselves," he said.

He also enters wood carving shows and competitions. Because chip carvers are scattered throughout the country, McKenzie is often the token chip carver competing. Not discouraged, he'll show duck makers, stick whittlers, and the browsers his creations. A lazy Susan, copied from a sunflower center, is so precisely carved it could be a clock, and his four-foot walking stick has won Best of Show.

His strategies have worked. His quarterly chip-carving newsletter has grown to 500 subscribers. Carvers from Italy, Sweden, South Africa, or Australia, where the craft is more popular, correspond with him. He now hosts a chip carver's conference every September.

"When I started, I was so new. I didn't know what I shouldn't do. I invented my own form," he said. Unlike other carvers who chip and varnish decorative plates and plaques in monotones, McKenzie cuts through stained or painted wood. He invented stencil veneers for birdhouses and Christmas ornaments.

"The first time I cut through the wood my teacher said, 'That's just not done.' I said, 'But I want to do that.'"

McKenzie decorates boxes for stamps or tissues, lamp stands, shelving, utensils or bowls much like chip carving began.

"In the 1400s, people couldn't afford to buy a painting," said Barbara McKenzie. "They could decorate the cabinets or useful objects with carving."

Though McKenzie willingly shares his ideas through newsletters and correspondence, he refuses to turn carving into an assembly-line affair.

"I don't want employees. I want to be in charge of everything. Not because I'm a control freak, but because I enjoy every part of it," he said.

In the afternoon, McKenzie settles into his living room armchair to carve. Alternating projects, he carves eight to ten hours a day on a banister facing, a Swedish lunch box, or decorative shelving.

"Once you've mastered this craft, it's so self-satisfying it's addictive," he said. "All those years at power plants I never had the feeling of completion. In chip carving, it's done when I say it's done—whether it's got two chips or a thousand chips. You have something to show that will be around for generations."

Free Day Away

Church Serves as Sunday Haven for Soldiers

E ach Sunday, two hundred and fifty Fort Leonard Wood soldiers flee the military. Boarding a fleet of white buses, they leave behind drill instructors, M-16 rifles, and spit-and-polish barracks for an afternoon at Tabernacle Baptist Church's Free Day Away program.

For some eighteen and nineteen-year-olds, freshly shorn

Every week, four hundred soldiers escape their basic training for a Sunday afternoon at Tabernacle Baptist Church. Since 1971 volunteers have provided a home-cooked meal, telephones, candy machines, and an evening service for recruits.

of hair and civilian life, it's the first time they've been away from the tight rein of the Army's Total Control basic training. Others, further into the Advanced Individual Training, may be returning on their regular pass.

"Our goal is two-fold," explained the Rev. Archie C. Conn. "We want to provide an outlet for those in training. We want them to be around lay people, have a home-cooked meal in a home atmosphere, and have a church different from the military chapels. And secondly, we want to reach as many as we can with the message of the Lord Jesus Christ."

Newcomers have a thirty minute orientation to the Free Day Away program and a short Bible study. Until dinner, they do something they couldn't do on base. They call their time their own.

Soldiers choose either to be driven on to Bennett Spring State Park or to stay in Lebanon. In town, the skating rink and bowling alley, two blocks from the church, are open for them. At the church, they can opt to sleep on pews in the sanctuary or do nothing. Many wait in line for a phone to call home—collect.

For Sean Kelly, a New Mexico recruit three weeks into his Army hitch, just leaning against the wall outside the church and drinking as many sodas as he pleased is nice. "Relaxation isn't part of a drill instructor's vocabulary," he explained wryly.

Some write letters or call girlfriends back home on church phones. They watch television in a recreation room, play volleyball, or football outside. Both soldiers still laced into fatigues and combat boots and AIT personnel who have shed uniforms for gym clothing play basketball at one end of the church's basketball court.

At the other end, church volunteers set tables for the meal. A full-time cook prepares the chicken-fried steak, corn, applesauce, potatoes and gravy. Rotating teams of ten women serve the meal or supply homemade pies and cakes. Holiday menus add watermelon and tomatoes in the summer or turkey and dressing in winter.

Since the Free Day Away project began Easter Sunday

Tabernacle Baptist Church volunteer Dan Street serves homeade dessert to Eric Long from Flint, Michigan.

1971, 80,000 to 100,000 soldiers have visited Tabernacle Baptist Church. Program coordinator Cliff Mizer works scheduling under the approval of the Fort's post and brigade chaplains.

Officers on base explain the Free Day Away to basic trainees who have earned their first pass. Activities are funded and manned on a donation/volunteer basis by members of the congregation. Designated a home mission outreach, the program's price tag is around $1,200 a week.

"Parents learn of the program and often write the church, asking it to contact their child," Conn said. One North Dakota couple met their son on the church grounds since he was not yet eligible for a regular pass.

Though the only cost to the soldiers is skating and bowling fees, they must conform to the church's expectations—no alcohol or drugs, no smoking on buses or church grounds, and no wandering away from the immediate vicinity without a church chaperone.

Soldiers are required to attend the evening church service. For some, it is the first time they have been in a Baptist church or listened to a Baptist preacher. It is the reason others come. Nineteen-year-old Lewis King from Miami, Florida, said, "I like it. It reminds me of my home church. I come to this church to worship."

Pastor Conn and his civilian congregation purposefully cater to the 250 soldiers seated center front. "The men are the main attraction in every service," he said. "The only thing they don't do is preach."

The resulting commotion teeters near chaos as the preacher asks men to call out their hometowns and states. The soldiers are encouraged to say a loud "Amen" when they agree with something. They respond with window-rattling parade unison when songs include the word or the leader throws good-natured barbs toward their military routine.

Familiar hymns, "Amazing Grace" and "Revive Us Again" are included in the group singing. Soldiers sing solos, play piano or guitar for special music. One young man volunteered his own composition, "The Power of God." They sometimes participate as ushers or alter workers at the ending of services.

They are the focus of each service's invitation to make a decision for Christ. "Many drill instructors are thrilled with the program," said Conn. "When a man makes a commitment to Christ, it changes his life. It also has a positive effect on those who do not. Drill instructors know that. Their job is easier."

The church often receives letters after the soldiers have been shipped out, expressing appreciation. Sometimes the "thank you" is more immediate. During a sharing time after the sermon, one young man stood up to say, "We from the Fort want to give you a hand for all you've done for us here today." The applause from this man's Army was thunderous.

Ozark Barrels Flavor the World

Independent Stave Company

When connoisseurs of wines and spirits tip their glasses skyward, what they taste is the sun, rain, soil, and wood of the Ozarks. Not exactly moonshine, but pure Ozarks just the same, for bourbon and wines acquire their preferred flavors from storage barrels made from the white oak of the Ozarks. Over half the world's barrels, notched as staves into an airtight seal, are manufactured by the Independent Stave

Subtle flavors and aromas produced by the white oak tree are enhanced by the toasting process at Independent Stave Company in Lebanon, Missouri. (Photos courtesy Independent Stave Company)

Company—the Lebanon-based company operated by four generations of the Boswell family.

The Tupperware of the past, the barrel's prehistoric prototype was just a hollowed out log with animal skins at each end. Later, Crusaders used the rounded wooden containers to bring back black gold—pepper—along with other spices from the Holy Land. During the Middle Ages, the barrel, with the King's liquor inside, was a sign of how seriously the sovereign took himself. In the United States, fish at the coastal ports, salt, flour, pickles, fruit for pioneer wagon trains, and soft drinks during Prohibition have also found their way inside the barrel.

But today, after the advent of aluminum foil and zip lock baggies, the barrel's primary use has narrowed to the aging of wines and spirits. As in the past, the fifty-three and fifty-nine gallon barrels begin in the forest. Cut from the Ozark region of the Midwest, the trees are the Quercus Alba species. The rocky soil and the unforgiving Ozark winters make a slow growth tree of straight, fine grains. At the sawmills, the logs are cut into blocks, just slightly longer than the finished stave (barrel sides) or heading (circular ends). The blocks, ranging from 17-46 inches, are cut into fourths and renamed as the bolt. The bolt is then cut into quarter inch thick staves.

Stacked outside, the staves are exposed to the fire and ice environment of the Ozarks weather. The staves, which are more than half moisture, are baked by the summer sun and blanched by winter's cold for up to two years. Drying the oak eliminates harsh and undesirable natural chemicals distasteful to the palate.

Once initially seasoned, the staves begin processing inside the factory in a dry kiln (for bourbon barrels) or pre-dryer (for wine barrels) Stoked by oak waste, the heat dries to a uniform level. The side staves are jointed and the heading circle is cut from the heading square. Another trial by fire (steam for bourbon staves) and dry heat (for wine staves) limbers the staves. Flaring like rays from the temporary holding hoops, the staves can bow into the correct barrel shape.

Then, things really heat up. A fifty-five second searing of the inside of the barrel caramelizes the wood sugars, which will later affect the color, aroma, and smoky flavors of the bourbon. Bourbon clients specify which of four different charring intensities they want. For a wine barrel, the process is a forty-five minute process over small oak chip pots. Fifteen different fires penetrate into layers of wood to avail the vanillin, sweet-toasting caramel and other spice flavorings to the wine barrels. The white oak wine barrel is still sealed with the traditional flour and water paste to avoid another chemical reaction with the liquor. The bourbon barrel is sealed with FDA approved geon sealant.

The alcohol is clear when poured through the bunghole into the barrel. Depending on distiller preference, it's left from two to twenty-eight years, seeping into the charred cracks and fissures to assume their color. A new charred white oak barrel makes official bourbon. A used barrel creates scotch. The flavors, from vanillin to cloves to cinnamon to chocolate to nutmeg, leach from the wood that grew eighty years from acorn to its thirteen-inch diameter. Wood barrels also breathe, permitting the evaporation of other undesirable components.

The process, now a blend of traditional past and present technology, began for the Boswell family in 1912 with T.W. Boswell and 1,000 acres of white oak forest near

Sommersvile, Missouri. Opening T.W. Boswell's Stave Company, he owned and brokered for thirty-six southern and Midwestern stave mills.

"In those days, old drum saws at the mills were powered by steam engines," said Amie Boswell, T.W Boswell's great granddaughter and now in charge of marketing communications. "Mills were *portable*, moving from forest to forest. Using strong Missouri mules, they dragged logs from the forests to the mills."

The barrels were primarily used for beer, though pickles, oil, and flour were also stored in them. So important was the barrel container to the populace that the total barrel production in 1929 exceeded twenty million barrels.

Perhaps key to the company's longevity is the Boswell ability to roll through adversity. Prohibition of 1920 dried up a large share of the barrel market. To survive, the firm shifted priorities to fruit, meat, salt and other non-alcoholic commodities.

When Prohibition ended, production rebounded. A white oak stave sold for one dollar, twenty times the cost of a loaf of bread. When T.W.'s son, James E., graduated from Georgia School of Technology in 1933, *and Son* was added to the name. Three years later, James E. branched out on his own, borrowing money from his mother and equipment from his father to start the Independent Stave Company in Lebanon, Missouri.

By 1951, stainless steel developed as preferred material for beer. James E. and Independent Stave, now the parent company for operations, shifted emphasis to bourbon barrels.

His son John, present CEO, established the World

"Raising" the barrel requires the proper selection of staves to be placed in the truss hoop.

Cooperage Company, a division of Independent Stave. He added 150,000 wine barrels to its production. This new direction developed, in part, from the publicity surrounding the possible health benefits from moderate wine consumption. Traveling in Europe, John visited French cooperages and adapted their techniques to his American oak cooperage.

In tandem with manufacturing barrels, John added *Barrels of Fun.* The store, located above the factory, offers tours of the barrel-making process.

"*At Barrels of Fun,* we showcase products aged in our barrels," said Amie. "It also educates the general public about barrel, wine and spirit industries in a hands-on approach."

The store sells, among others, Jim Beam, Wild Turkey, Seagram's 7 Crown, and Old Grand Dad, along with the wines of Missouri, California's Sonoma and Napa Valleys, Spain, Italy, and Australia.

Though now mechanized and automated, manufacturing the barrel from its once-living components is not an automatic accomplishment. "It's a natural product," Amie explained. "It's not always going to bend like it's supposed to. We have skilled and experienced associates who know how to work with wood. Believe it or not, a good sense of smell is required for toasting barrels, similar to making wine. They want sweet, soft aromas, not burnt ones."

Spurred on by the market to export it for flooring and furniture in Europe and Asia, white oak wood is at a premium. Nothing is wasted.

"We throw absolutely nothing away," said Amie. "We use every bit of the tree. We're very efficient. By-products are converted into decorative mulch or composted into chips for pulp or fuel. We also sell the sawdust to Kingsford charcoal for briskets."

Over a twenty-year period, the barrel itself can be recycled as many as ten times, flavoring differing spirits for varying time lengths. After making straight whiskey, light whiskey, tequila, gin, rum, or scotch, some barrels are then exported for use in Europe or sold to nurseries for planters.

Independent Stave's 600,000 barrels a year now accounts for over half the market for the white oak barrels. The company has five stave mills in the United States as well as Monthureaux, France. Ten log buying yards in Missouri and Kentucky supply their two barrel factories in Lebanon, Missouri and Lebanon, Kentucky. In total, both facilities can produce over 4,000 barrels per day. Sales personnel in South America, Europe, Chile, and Australia market their barrels. Experiments to refine their product are conducted in Scotland.

The Boswell family, now four generations from the company's beginning, manage the company. "It's always business," said Amie. "Nonstop. We are a driven family. We eat, live, and breathe the barrel business. That's what makes it a success."

Styrofoam, Saran Wrap, Corning Ware and plastics may have replaced the barrels' storage usefulness in today's microwave society, but they will never be able to contain the great outdoors. For that, depend on the white oak barrel and an Ozark company that makes it.

The Ozarks in a Pot

David G. Massey

David Massey shows Marshall Jones the miniature tree he's growing in a bonsai pot. (Photo courtesy of Veda Boyd Jones)

Bonsai—nature in a pot. When David Massey creates his little trees, they're living haiku. Following the ancient process, the owner of Ozark Bonsai Nursery duplicates the Asian masters with a local touch. He dwarfs native materials to recreate what's just outside the window.

"What I try to make is a replica of the Ozark landscape," Massey said. "I mound the dirt up to represent the rolling hills, put in gravel for a gravel bar, and use native rock to recreate rock outcroppings and bluffs."

In the space of a chafing dish, he can fashion multiple-plant bonsai to resemble a forest clearing. His rock, tree, and moss combinations repeat what glaciers took eons to make.

Massey's miniature masterpieces are made with common Ozark redbud, mulberry, elm, wisteria, Virginia creeper and juniper. Because its white flowers and blue berries bloom first in the spring, he often uses serviceberry. Massey finds his plants in twelve acres of undergrowth behind his Lacamo Landscaping business or growing wild in his mother's flowerbed or along bluffs on his friends' properties.

"Even when I'm hiking in the woods, I have my eyes peeled for prospects. I'm looking for small trees, stunted by nature," he explained.

He continually searches for something unusual in the trunk or branch structure. A bulge, a split, or a scar in the trunk is an ideal focal point in developing a bonsai tree. The twenty-five year veteran landscaper then leaves the plant with the 400-500 others in his open-air greenhouse.

Creating a bonsai tree takes patience and time. For three years Massey waits for the plant to recover from being moved. It's a slow process. He prunes back the taproot so that fine root hairs can develop a dense root system able to support the tree in the shallow bonsai pot.

Made of stoneware to resist cracking during the winter, the traditional dishes are one-half to three inches deep. Once

in the pot, the bonsai can grow into one of twelve traditional formations. Massey may brush off the dirt and loop a root
tentacle over a rock. Using string or wire, he gently coaxes
the branches into cascades over the lip of the pot or trains the
trunk into an off-center curve. He may prune back unwant-
ed branches to expose the front trunk. He meticulously clips
each leaf or needle until the canopy thickens and sweeps
toward the back of the bonsai tree.

"It takes two to three years to get past the rough stage,"
he said. "It should look like a real tree in miniature and not
something just slapped in a pot," he said. Normally, he
spends five years completing his Ozark bonsai.

Bonsai began about 206 B.C. Artisans went to the mountain tree line to find stunted pines and beeches to place in
shallow dishes. As nature's supply diminished, the Chinese
discovered methods of dwarfing the trees artificially.

Bonsai grow from eight inches to three feet high. In his
Ozark landscapes, Massey can group trees in a large pot or on
flat limestone. By placing the smaller plants in the back of the
grove, Massey recreates nature's perspective. He also pots
juniper or bird's nest spruce individually to display their
shape.

"You get attached after working with them so extensive-
ly," he said. His prize bonsai, a fifty-year-old hornbeam, was
rescued from a customer who wanted it dug out of her lawn.
Cutting back its top growth, he found a blackened concave
scar.

"I saw the possibilities of the trunk," he said. He'd sell it
for $1,500, but not a penny less. Other bonsai, for which he
has less affection, are priced from twenty dollars, depending
on the tree's age and the amount of time he's invested into it.

Once purchased, bonsai are not meant to be house-bound or held captive by hothouse glass. They should be enjoyed outside on a balcony patio or deck from early spring to early frost.

"Since some of their roots are exposed, they should be wintered in an unheated porch or garage. Or, if you can heel them in the ground with straw and leave the top exposed, they'll survive," said Massey. But he cautions against bringing them into a living room environment.

"I think of these little plants like pets that you feed and water and groom," said Massey. "You water them daily, feed them with liquid fertilizer weekly, and then prune. They respond. They grow lush, look healthy, and make a beautiful plant."

"It's peaceful work," he said. "There is something ethere-al about working with these trees. You should spend time with them every day, caring for them, fussing over them and grooming them. They have a soothing, calming effect. After you're done, you'll be refreshed. Bonsai were created for spir-itual reasons," Massey said. "They reminded the monks of their place in the cosmos. As a miniature form of a natural scene, they helped them to mediate, to define their relation-ship to God."

Pulitzer Prize Playwright
Remembers the Ozarks

Lanford Wilson

"*Tally's Folly* is a valentine. I hope the people of Lebanon leave the theater thinking that love is possible to everyone," said Lanford Wilson.

Folly earned Wilson a Pulizer Prize. It is second in a trilogy

chronicling the Talley Family and Lebanon, Missouri, the playwright's hometown. The first play, *The Fifth of July*, ran on Broadway, starring Christopher Reeve (Superman) and Richard Thomas (The Waltons). The trilogy concludes with *A Tale Told*.

Lanford Wilson won a Pulitzer Prize for Talley's Folly, *a drama set in his hometown of Lebanon, Missouri. (Photo courtesy Christian County Museum)*

Folly turns on Matt Friedman's pursuit of Sally Talley, the girl he wants to marry. Sally's snobbish and wealthy parents oppose the match to the German Jew, but during a Fourth of July evening at the family boathouse, he captures her heart.

"*Talley's Folly* is the most positive and romantic thing I've ever written," Wilson said. "Many of my plays are abrasive and hard-edged with strong social comment. This play is mainly a love story of two vaguely social outcasts."

"I think *New York Post* drama critic Clive Barnes said it best when he said, '*Talley's Folly* is a love story between an apple and an orange.' I wouldn't think of making them an ideal couple, but the more you know them, the more you know they're absolutely right for each other."

Other Missouri landmarks included in Wilson's work are Bennett Spring and the Niangua and the Gasconade rivers. An unlikely, but romantic, Victorian boathouse is located on the water's bank in his drama.

"I lived in Lebanon until I was five and spent summers there until I was thirteen," Wilson recounted. "I had a really nice early childhood experience there. Lebanon has a very romantic feeling for me."

Wilson said his original intention was to incorporate a strong religious undertow in *Talley's Folly*. He said he liked the Biblical name of Lebanon. Although the religious sub-theme was replaced later in favor of social and economic underpinnings, Wilson said, the name stuck.

"The people in the play are a composite of people I knew from Branson, Ozark, and Springfield. I was brought up on the wrong side of the tracks in Old Town, and I didn't know anyone really wealthy. So, I thought it was all right to use Lebanon."

To assist actress Helen Stenborg in her portrayal of 64-

year-old Aunt Sally Friedman in *The Fifth of July* in 1978, Wilson composed a biography of Sally's husband Matt and pictured actor Judd Hirsch (of the television series *Taxi*). *Talley's Folly* grew from this acting aid.

The *Fifth of July* is set thirty-three years after Sally and Matt declare their love. Kenny, Sally's nephew, has lost both legs in Vietnam. He owns the Talley farm but wants to sell it. Six houseguests enter, some who are aging California activists. Wilson said the play has "a strong forward thrust" in a theme concerning "what you can take from your past and use in your life."

A *Tale Told*, which Wilson formerly called *The War in Lebanon*, takes place just before and after the 1966 night of *Talley's Folly*. The scene has shifted away from the boathouse to the hill. "The new play," said Wilson, "is a much more dangerous play, more abrasive. It's about rich people in the process of a power struggle to control the family. It has to do with the death of a patriarch who has controlled the family for sixty-seventy years. And it has to do with dispersing enormous wealth—by Lebanon standards.

Bits and Pieces of Harold Bell Wright
Eric Tudor

Forget the Sammy Lane spoons; ignore Old Matt's log cabin syrup containers; pass by the *Shepherd of the Hills* coffee cups and tin boxes. Eric Tabor is a paper man. Books, posters, postcards, player piano rolls, sheet music, and stationery are his treasure. Each bookmark and movie playbill, every photograph and letter are stamped with the

Eric Tudor regards To My Sons, *not* Shepherd of the Hills, *as the most valuable item in his Harold Bell Wright collection.*

Ozark legend, Harold Bell Wright.

The Lebanon resident has been acquiring Harold Bell Wright memorabilia for fifteen years and is one of the top collectors of Wright mementos. Tudor's collection fills a room in his two-story Victorian home. Its monetary value could buy a house; its historical worth is priceless.

"My mother bought the book that started this disease," said Tudor. "She got *The Calling of Dan Matthews* for about fifty cents at a garage sale. Her goal was to have a full set of his books. It was just natural for me to help."

Then Tudor caught the virus, too.

"When she had all nineteen, she was content," said Tudor. "Her collecting came to a standstill, but mine had just started. I had come upon several interesting advertising items. There is so much more on the other side of the books."

Besides autographed first editions, Tudor's collection encompasses the marketing genius of Wright's publisher, Elsbery Reynolds. "He was a master in advertising," said Tudor. "He came up with different concepts no one else had done before."

Tudor has full-page ads which Reynolds placed in Sears, Roebuck catalogs, *The Saturday Evening Post*, *Companion for Youth*, and *Cosmopolitan Magazine*. He also has special Christmas edition dust jackets, boxed sets, and specially designed author's advance copies for bookstores. Tudor's photograph of Wright, his wife, and three boys was part of Reynolds' promotion on *The Eyes of the World*. To obtain it, customers had to buy the book before its publication date. "He was snagging orders even before the book was out," said Tudor.

Reynolds featured Wright's books prominently in his book supply catalog, giving Wright full-page promotions rather than sharing space with other authors. He encouraged purchasers to tell others about Wright by inserting post cards, complete with order form, in each book. Part of Tudor's four-hundred card collection is devoted to these post-cards.

Though *Shepherd of the Hills* remains the watermark of Wright's career, Tudor's prize possession is a copy of *To My Sons*. It was written when declining health and declining book sales affected Wright's career. "It's the most valuable book out of the entire collection," said Tudor of his nine auto-graphed first editions.

Another of his high dollar items is a rare photograph of the writer, which is not for sale at any price. An elderly woman who learned of Tudor's interest in Wright gave it to Tudor. "It's a 1892 school photo taken at Hiram College in Ohio," he said. "His family doesn't even have one like it."

Though many remember him only as the stiff and stern minister, captured in formal portraits, the Harold Bell Wright in Eric Tudor's collection also owned a swimming pool, rode horses, and owned a movie studio. Tudor's eighteen movie posters track the Hollywood hype surrounding Wright's life in the West. His titles, in large capital letters, spread across three feet of poster boards. *The Recreation of Bryan Kent, The Calling of Dan Matthews, The Mine with the Iron Door, When a Man's a Man,* and *Shepherd of the Hills.* The movie stars, Ronald Coleman, Ralph Bellamy, and John Wayne smile just above Wright's name.

"He helped two major film stars begin their careers," said Tudor. "It's well known that John Wayne's first major role was in *Shepherd of the Hills.*"

As co-director of *The Winning of Barbara Worth,* Wright objected to an actor looking too much like a city slicker.

"Wright said that he didn't walk like a cowboy or look like a cowboy," said Tudor. "Then Wright noticed a tall, gangly guy who was leaning against a rail fence. Wright said, 'Now that guy looks like a cowboy.' It turned out to be Gary Cooper and getting the part was his first major role."

Tudor's continued interest in movie memorabilia has unreeled into a mini-collection—a player piano roll that goes with the sheet music that corresponds to the movie that was written about the book, *When a Man's a Man*.

His postcards also picture Wright's Arizona home, designed after Pueblo Indian dwellings. He stayed with the Papago Indians who Tudor discovered gave him the Indian name, "Pungee" which Wright used to autograph some of his books.

"He loved cowboys and Indians," Tudor said. "He'd take guests out to camp in the rocks and bluffs. That was his idea of a good time—going out and baking in the desert."

Tudor has postcards showing the home and its rare cactus garden. They also capture the interior of the opulent Barbara Worth Hotel in El Centro, California, and catch the author posing for its mural size pictures. Tudor owns a menu from that hotel, as well as Barbara Worth fruit and vegetable orange crate labels. The two-story structure with its ornate ceilings and arches were a long way from Old Matt's cabin in the Ozarks.

Still, the most valuable of Tudor's postcards depicts two famous real-life characters from *Shepherd of the Hills* country. Tudor has an early 1920s photo of beardless Uncle Ike, a photo of Pearl "Sparky" Spurlock, the taxicab driver who was the first tour agent in Branson, and a photo of Old Matt's Cabin before the chimney was added.

Besides sketches of Wright's thatch-roofed writing cabin, pamphlets from his church sermon notes and stationery, Tudor has issues of *Ladies Home Journal, Saturday Evening Post,* and *Physical Culture for Mind and Body.* In them, Wright sermonized "What about God?" and serialized "The Devil's Highway." "Why I Did Not Die" appears in *The American Magazine,* June 1924, a story retelling of Wright's mugging by teenagers.

Tudor searches through both old and new sources. He scrounges through flea markets, bookstores, and annually heads through Iowa and Minnesota antique stores. New York is a good resource because New Yorkers had money to buy books and magazines. Branson and Springfield areas are rich in Wright memorabilia. Tudor also posts his ad on the Internet. He barters and trades with other serious collectors in Ohio, Kansas, Arizona, and California to upgrade his pieces. He's bought and sold an advertisement of the first silent black and white version of *Shepherd of the Hills* four times. His current one is in pristine condition, with only the original crease in the center marking it.

Some memorabilia voluntarily comes to Tudor. "My name has gotten around," he said. "A lady in town (Lebanon) gave me a pamphlet Wright passed out to his congregation. She said, 'I've got no use for it, but I know you'll take care of it.'"

So Eric Tudor keeps accepting scraps of paper, tissue thin or board thick. He gathers up personal letters, stereo view cards, movie lobby cards, and tablet notebooks.

"I've come across so many people who love Harold Bell Wright. I hope to spark new interest and breathe new life into old collections."

Ozark Values on the Federal Bench

Judge Dean Whipple

On weekends, Dean Whipple is one of the good ol' boys. He likes his Coors cold, his cards poker, and his hunting deep in the woods. But, come Monday mornings he hangs up his cowboy hat and dons judicial black. Under the Great Seal of the United States and to the right of the U.S. flag, the Chief United States district court judge likes his jury

"I'm trying to bring Ozark common sense to the inricacies of federal litigation," says U.S. District Judge Dean Whipple. (Photo by Jeff Joiner, Rural Missouri)

informed, his attorneys concise, and his docket fully scheduled.

Since 1982, Whipple's domain has been the federal court building in Kansas City. His authority is as wide as the U.S. Constitution itself and as narrow as the conservatism with which he interprets it. He runs his court like his life—direct and to the point. "I'm trying to bring Ozark common sense to the intricacies of federal litigation," he said.

No old money eased him into his federal career. Born and raised in Lebanon, he watched his father run his sheet metal business in the outbuilding behind the family home. In the summers, Whipple helped out. His blue-collar family life and his father shaped his values.

"My dad was authoritarian," said Whipple. "He set the example and instilled in me what was expected. He taught me to be a man of my word."

Whipple's rise was as jagged as a rail fence and just as splintered. He began as a gangly freshman whose ambitions didn't include lawyering. At Springfield's Drury College, Whipple aspired to be an automotive engineer. His studies, however, were ambushed by dorm life. "Smoking and drinking interfered with my engineering program," Whipple said. "I sunk down to academic probation. It was nothing more than I didn't study."

Switching majors, Whipple graduated in 1961 with a degree in business and economics. Realizing his degree was too generic, he headed for the only graduate school without a minimum grade point average—law.

Whipple's graduate school education began with midterm enrollment at the University of Missouri where the admissions office decreed he'd have to take second semester courses without fundamentals from the first.

"I'm from the country, but I wasn't dumb," said Whipple with his typical forthrightness. "I couldn't learn a whole semester's case law in three weeks."

Rather than flunk out, Whipple returned to Lebanon to grease cars, until he discovered the University of Tulsa's night law school. With a full-time job during the day, he attended classes at night and slept on weekends. Later Whipple transferred his night school credits to the University of Missouri-Kansas City School of Law where he graduated in 1965.

Mementos decorate Whipple's chambers and chronicle his private practice in Lebanon and Camdenton, his four-year stint as Laclede County prosecuting attorney, and his election as a judge for Missouri's 26th Judicial Circuit, where he presided for thirteen years.

A finalist in 1981 and 1982, Whipple was appointed as a federal judge by President Reagan in 1987. Overseeing the Western District's sixty-six counties, his jurisdiction covers two-thirds of Missouri, including Kansas City, Springfield, Joplin, St. Joseph, and Jefferson City.

Inheriting a backlog of four hundred cases, Whipple set early trial dates to nudge cases into court, limiting lawyers to nine months' preparation. He also "stacked" cases, scheduling several back-to-back on the same date so another began if one settled out of court.

"The bottom line is that they didn't put me in this job because I was a shirker," said Whipple. "They believed I would try cases and move my docket. I developed a reputation as a conscientious judge." Typically Whipple gives taxpayers their money's worth. He parks his car downtown at 7:15 a.m. Between trials and during recesses, he writes opinions, reads briefs, and returns messages. Ten hours later he leaves his chambers and the piles of manila folders that detail his 250 pending cases.

By random draw, Whipple tends several ongoing controversies. Since 1983, he's managed Jackson County Foster Care, periodically imposing contempt charges for neglecting to lower caseloads or improve training procedures. He seized the Kansas City Pubic Housing Authority for failing to rehabilitate housing projects or show where tax dollars were spent. He monitors Jackson County's overcrowded jails.

"The federal court should not manage the jail or foster care," he said. "But, I'm doing it because the state is not."

Whipple's conservatism stands out like the starched white of his dress shirts. In a world of gray nuances, he consistently retraces existing case law rather than influence, by opinion, social issues. His gavel falls heavy on the unrepentant. With one eyebrow cocked toward attitude, Whipple said, "I will always impose longer sentences when there is no acknowledgment of guilt or expression of remorse."

He sentenced Springfield's Trula Walker to more years for tax evasion than Al Capone was sentenced. Willie Aiken, one-time Kansas City Royal, is serving twenty years for dealing drugs. "He never admitted his guilt," said Whipple.

With a lifetime appointment, Whipple answers only to the federal court of appeals and the U.S. Supreme Court. "I want to do the best job I can and be supported by the appellate court," he said. "I don't want a reputation for being reversed."

"It's respect for the legal system," he explained of his benevolent handling of juries and tight-fisted control of lawyers. Attorney's expect a willow-switch tongue lashing if they stray from his two-page guideline on protecting witnesses and efficiently presenting cases.

"Sometimes big-city lawyers think because I'm from the country, they can get something on me. I tell them, 'I've been doing this for several decades. If you tell a story I haven't heard, I'll congratulate you in court.' Since I'm plain spoken and direct, I expect people to conduct themselves in a straightforward manner. They should get to the point."

Presiding above the fray, Whipple relishes the trials' mental challenge and shadow boxing with attorneys. "I didn't go to college to be a lawyer. I didn't go to law school to be a judge. I didn't become a state judge to become a federal judge," he said in his Ozark drawl. "It all fell into place because I found the great niche of the law. I am a student of it and will be the rest of my life."

Justice may be blind, but His Honor, Dean Whipple, is not. On balance, his scales swing evenly between city slicker sophistication and Ozark country simplicity. A common man in an uncommon job, he knows exactly who he is and where he comes from.

The
Lights of

RICHLAND, FT. LEONARD WOOD, STEELVILLE, AND JEFFERSON CITY

Jigsaw Puzzle Fun

Nancy and Keith Ballhagen

I t's a store full of bits and pieces. A piece of laughter here. A giggle there. A smile in the corner. Nancy Ballhagen's Puzzles at Sleeper Junction and Interstate 44 is a building full of good-time entertainment to take home.

Nancy Ballhagen holds a 350-piece jigsaw fiddle. She offers over 2200 different puzzles in her store, just off the Sleeper Exit (Exit 135) east of Lebanon.

"I can tell what they're laughing at by where they are in the store," said Nancy Ballhagen of the customers who pull up the gravel drive to her unique roadside business.

For a decade, Nancy and Keith Ballhagen have been putting the pieces together in an apparent one-of-a-kind enterprise along the interstate.

Their puzzle exclusive store carries 1,761 designs ranging from traditional animals to landscapes to three-dimensional to puzzles-within-a-puzzle challenges to Star Trek holograms.

"The puzzle that sells the best is scenery," Nancy said. "But a lot of people like sea life—whales, dolphins, that kind of thing. Every once in a while we're inundated with mills, covered bridges, barns."

They've sold puzzles, exclusively—both commercially made and custom designed—since 1989. After relocating from California, they began their puzzle business with sixty boxes and a sign in the yard. They have since sold several thousand puzzles.

"We had customers the first day," Nancy recalled. Relying on three billboards and word-of-mouth, the Ballhagens have built a clientele on vacationers and passers-by. People on their way to Branson turn off at Sleeper (Exit 135) east of Lebanon. Their customers may pull up in a semi-truck en route to delivering lumber or with a trailer full of exotic rabbits.

"Once a person stops, they'll come by again and again," she said. As if to prove the point, a couple comes into the store, on their way back from California to Chicago. While buying five puzzles, they admit they've been customers for five years. "I don't know of any store that sells jigsaw puzzles exclusively. Most places are like Toys R Us, Wal-Mart, and gift shops."

The 4 x 8 1/2 foot panoramic view of New York City Harbor the Ballhagens put together themselves really started it all. The

7500-piece puzzle began as a holiday activity for company.

"We put it together the first Christmas we were here—when my mother and our son were visiting," said Nancy. "Most of it was done in two and a half weeks. When we got to the sky, all the company went home, and our help dropped out. We had it on the table ten months."

Though framed and displayed on the front wall of the store, it can be purchased for one hundred dollars by avid puzzle advocates. It, along with the replica of the Sistine Chapel, is the top dollar item in the store. For the less ambitious, other puzzles and prices diminish down to fifty-four pieces and ninety-nine cent fare.

Browsing through aisles stacked to the ceiling is fun. The puzzles become more than a mere putting together pieces of cardboard Americana. To be sure, Americana is there—in Norman Rockwell puzzles, American Indian scenes, and Charles Wysocki primitive drawings of country life. "The general store, painted with the ever all-American red trademark of the Coca-Cola company is one of the best sellers," she said.

There is more complexity to these puzzles than the visual challenge of finding a specific piece from the jumble of 300 to 7,000 others on the card table and locking it into place. The "Impossibles" series, for example, increases the level of difficulty by eliminating the borders and including five extra pieces that don't belong in the puzzle. Today's jigsaw puzzles also offer mental challenges. Some, called "Mysteries," come with a short story in which a murder is committed.

"Shop 'til You Drop," "Death by Diet,"or "Ghost of Winthrup," come without sample picture. Clues in the completed puzzle lead to solving the murder mystery. Other puzzles may challenge the puzzler to find 1,000 objects in the picture that begins with the letter "S" or to identify fifteen characters at "The Dinner Party."

In "North American Prairie Vanishing Vistas," the puzzler must identity one hundred plants and animals in the completed picture. The object of another is to find sixty movie titles in the cartoon drawings the puzzle has made. M.C. Escher's optical illusions come in regular size puzzles or in a 2 1/2-inch square featuring ninety-nine interlocking pieces just one-eighth inch big.

For those who seek cultural enhancement while relaxing, several companies offer museum puzzles, some of which are replicas by famous painters—Monet, Dahli, Picasso, Homer, and Bruegal. A "Buried Blueprints" line is linked to the "Egyptian Chronicles" or "King Solomon's Mines."

Titles of some puzzles are a play on words. "Butts are Gross," details the tail end of selected animals, and the "Nature Calls" series has two versions of outhouses—one is international in theme—the other features outhouses of the mountains (mostly in the East). Matching playing cards and earrings (complete with occupants enthroned in the tiny structure) are available. A "Santa Claws" features cats in holiday hats, and its companion "Santa Paws" spotlights dogs. "Minnesota Cats" naturally places the cat next to a pool table.

Besides the sports, fantasy, and World War II sections, the Ballhagens keep a special category devoted to Missouri. They special ordered scenes of the St. Louis Arch, Eads Bridge, and Union Station. Cartoon puzzles feature the old Sportsman Park, the Chiefs, and road map puzzles of Kansas City and St. Louis. Members of the Route 66 Club, the Ballhagens also created a large montage of Route 66 memorabilia. "We have a puzzle for everybody," Nancy said. "It can be anything."

Nancy orders inventory from forty-five different companies

and puzzles from eleven countries, including Spain, England, France, Austria, Mexico, and Switzerland. The puzzles from abroad have more pieces, usually over 3,000. Only one company, Milton-Bradley in the United States, makes large puzzles. "Originally jigsaw puzzles came from Europe," Nancy said. "They are more serious about it over there than we are."

Besides the imported puzzles with a large number of pieces, the Ballhagens have some puzzles with mechanical inner workings. One is a grandfather clock that can be hung on the wall and used as a clock. Others include puzzles that come complete with frames and tiny lights that illuminate "Amsterdam at Night" and the "Bavarian Village Christmas."

The Ballhagens are open seven days a week, fifty weeks a year. Though their best season is in summer; November is busy for Christmas shopping. "We're here at seven thirty and try to go home at five o'clock," Nancy said. "Since we built this building, all our business is in here. We used to keep things in the house, but now we want to go home like everybody else—to watch TV or do a puzzle. We kind of like them. Doing puzzles is relaxing. It take the edge off."

To replenish inventory, Nancy orders twice a year. Victorian settings, guardian angel images, Precious Moments beauties, and the Christmas-holiday fare are popular items. The Ballhagens sometimes find it difficult to correctly guess customers' preference. "Luke Perry of 90210 took us three years to sell," said Nancy. "Eventually they all seem to sell."

Besides the commercial puzzles, the Ballhagens make two kinds of custom puzzles themselves. Keith and Nancy use posters, art prints, record covers, and calendar pictures to design their own puzzles. They glue the picture to wood and then free-hand cut the pieces in the small shop at the back of the store.

Their son, Richard, reproduces color photographs into eleven-inch rounds, eight by ten rectangles, and eleven by sixteen rectangles.

"His style includes figural cutting," his mother said. "He cuts some pieces as bats and guitars. In a Norman Rockwell print, "Saying Grace," he included an axe, an elephant, and other objects."

Keith Ballhagen may have summed up their hobby-business enterprise correctly. He said, "We're making order out of chaos. We dump the pieces out in a pile and then make a picture out of it."

Barbecue, Caveman Style

David and Connie Hughes

I t's not the ribs. Man has been gnawing on them since time began. It's where he ate the ribs when time began that makes the adventure. Caveman Bar-BQ and Steak House is located forty feet up the bluff and sixty more feet above the Gasconade River. And there, in a cave where man once rocked on his haunches, dinner is waiting.

The meal with-

The limestone ceiling and walls in Caveman Bar-BQ and Steakhouse was made by Mother Nature. The rest Dave and Connie Hughes made.

in the mountain is located near Richland, Missouri. Its three-level dining room curves where the current cut eons ago. Seating two hundred at red-checkered tablecloths and cafe booths, it winds 120 feet into the Ozark terrain and arches seventy feet wide. Poxed with ledges, cracks, and crevices, the walls and ceiling were formed by nature. The rest David and Connie Hughes made.

"About ten minutes after we took possession, a neighbor told us the cave held a dance hall in the twenties," Dave recalled of the turtle shell cave above their retirement property. "I put the jeep up against the cliff, leaned a ladder on top of it, and shined a flashlight into the forty-foot opening. I told Connie, 'Honey, we could build a restaurant up here.' She laughed so hard we just about fell off the cliff."

She had good reason to be amused. The potential for the restaurant was there, but it was buried under two feet of cave rubbish. Three quarters of a century old, the dance floor had fallen in. Only a one-foot space separated ceiling from solid rock beyond it.

Determined to forge ahead, Dave dug in. Using old-fashioned hard work, he unearthed his dream. "For four years, I jack hammered six hours a day. Then, we'd haul rock until eleven o'clock at night," he said of the one hundred sixty tons of debris they removed from the cave by shovel. Dave built a kitchen below the cave entrance and stacked a glass deck and balcony atop it. He washed down the walls with fire hoses. With Connie and the kitchen staff, he cleaned the cracks with brushes and garden tools. He poured five inches of concrete to level the floor and camouflaged the dehumidifier system (and the nine pounds of water it hourly sucked from the cave air) with two small waterfalls. When rain run-off dripped from a hole in the ceiling, Dave built a pool underneath it. He stocked it with goldfish and hybrid

blue gill which children now feed. "It just didn't make sense to mess with nature and try to glue something up," he said.

Depending on his ingenuity, the former Norwood farmer overcame the difficulties of a construction site too high above the bottom of Turkey Ridge and too far below its top to be reachable. He refused to accept that ten days and $10,000 would be required to position the deck's steel rafters. Instead he,

A meal in a mountain waits forty feet above the road, a hundred feet above the Gasconade River.

his wife, and a sixteen-year-old friend from church did it themselves. While they lowered the beams from an overhanging tree with come-along fence stretchers and a twenty-foot length of chain, Dave tiptoed across the beams to weld them in place. He concocted a dumb waiter, motored by two garage openers, and a motorcycle chain to transport food from the kitchen to the tables.

The restaurant's decor includes remnants from the five hundred acre farm the couple left. Using 1938 Chalmers tractor axles, Dave placed a half dozen lights along the curve of the rock ledges. He circled the chandelier with horseshoes that once belonged to his quarter horse and the neighbor's Tennessee Walker. He designed the balcony's iron railing and the four-foot window gratings from wrenches, cream separators, maddock spikes, a shoe lasp, wedge hammers, and wagon wheels.

"A lot of things from the farm ended up being used here," said Dave. "People give me things, or I buy them at yard sales and flea markets. I'm going to build a light out of brass blow torches next."

Dave positioned wildlife models on ledges or placed them where they would peek from tunnels in the wall. A turkey (with a four-foot wing span), a hornet's nest, antlers, raccoons, and photos of Caveman's four-year construction provide diversions for diners waiting for dinner. The deck's wrap-a-round balcony offers a panoramic view of the Gasconade River below.

The restaurant today specializes in barbecue and prime rib. Dave custom orders his meat from a local packer and cooks and tenderizes the turkey, brisket, and ham in his personally designed smoker. The restaurant specializes in an exotic food combo featuring emu, alligator, rattlesnake, and buffalo as well as a plate dinner of tame rabbit, quail, and pheasant on wild rice. No alcohol or diet drink is served; smoking is not allowed.

Connie and Dave added a personal touch to their homemade, Caveman bread. They bake the bread in stovepipe pans, copies of the ones Dave fashioned in the early days when they, as Dave said, were "poorer than snakes" on their farm and couldn't afford store-bought glass utensils.

Getting to Caveman is another part of the adventure. The route is easy enough on Interstate 44, but only one billboard advertises the place. More helpful is the 150-mile marker near Richland. Just off the 150 exit ramp, Highway W parallels the Interstate for a few yards and then meanders four miles past the water tower obelisk and the village of Turkey Ridge. The asphalt makes a dead end at a gravel lane. After a left turn and a single mile toward the river, a small white sign tacked on a tree base points the way into the ruts of the Ozark Springs Resort parking lot. Dave takes over the last quarter mile. From the parking lot, he drives guests up the bumpy ride and crooked gravel path toward the Cave, his vehicle careening past primitive log cabins and the fishermen staying there. A rock bluff on the left and a straight drop to the river on the right permanently define the route. The final forty feet takes a half-minute in the elevator Dave built and lined with Montana cedar. Dave estimated that he drove 35,000 people up the hill in the first eight months. "I took on this little resort because I wanted a place to go fishing. Now I can't get away," said Dave of his initial 1987 investment.

Caveman Bar-BQ early on exceeded Dave's five-year expectations. The couple spends evenings, five to nine, Tuesday through Friday, in their underground enterprise. They open up Saturday and Sunday at 11 a.m.

Connie manages the restaurant. David, dressed in baseball cap and sweatshirt, chauffeurs customers to the cave and back. He likes the driver's seat.

"That's how I know how my restaurant's doing," he said. "They don't know who I am. I know how my people feel when I put them on and when I take them off. Any complaints and I know about it."

His clientele discover Caveman through word-of-mouth and travel by any means to eat there. "I had a farmer from Ames hire a pilot to fly his family up and then back the same night," he recalled. A Kansas City couple made the trip in successive evenings with two different sets of friends in their van.

"I'm not a restaurateur. I'm just a farmer," Dave disclaimed. "I know how to work, and my wife knows quality when she sees it. It's the combination of her brains and my ability to build anything I can imagine that makes us a team."

Limestone, sandstone, and chirt arc overhead. Light softly shadows the walls. Aroma of fresh bread and smoked meat drift through the restaurant. Created by a trio of partners—Dave Hughes, Connie Hughes, and Mother Nature—Caveman's Bar-BQ and Steak House more than fits the bill.

The Big Picture

U.S. Army Engineer Museum

It's the size that intimidates. Usually war is captured magazine size and caught in photos of tiny tanks and little paratroopers. Children miniaturize the scenes in safe and manageable comic books, reducing combat to "Zap!" and "Pow!" in

cartoon frames. On the evening news, six-inch figures sprawl across the television screen, a comfortable and antiseptic room-length from our easy chair.

Not so at Fort Leonard

Near the end of Basic Training, Mark Daniel (fore-ground), tours the museum with Abbie, his wife, Jere Hines, his mother, and her husband, Steve.

Wood's U.S. Army Engineer Museum. There, war is bigger than life. Real life bridges fold across the lawn, leaving shadows large enough to drive a car through. Inside the building, the story of war, and the engineers who fought it, spreads into four galleries. A parachute hangs from the ceiling, a canopy over a stocky mannequin in full battle array. A swastika flag is pinned at eye level on the wall. The blood red background assaults the eye. A Japanese flag with its smear of human blood resides next to it. The rubble of history, like the remains of a bombed-out town, spills out in front of the displays, as if glass cannot hold it and distance cannot be maintained.

"We call them interpretations," said Fred Russ, Museum Curator and Director. "We take certain facts and tell a story with the exhibits and artifacts. We don't want just an open storage with Aunt Wilhelmena's cup sitting on a shelf."

This is true of the largest of the Museum's four galleries. Proceeding chronologically from 1775, the exhibits and dioramas show the contributions of military engineering from the Revolutionary War, through the Civil War, Reconstruction, World War II, Korea, Vietnam and Desert Storm conflicts.

A European cafe opens into the walkway. The 19th century pontoon wagon towers over the onlooker. Around the corner, a radioman sends signals from the underground trench. Gigantic "X's" litter the museum's reproduction of a beach at Normandy; and jungle growth replicates the rain forests of Vietnam.

The encyclopedic gallery explains the task engineers perform in the specialties of topographic engineering, land mine warfare, tactical bridging, explosives, and armaments.

The walkways curve through displays of the paraphernalia used by engineers in each category of service. The three-person staff Russ heads continually brainstorms innovative ways to emphasize American military engineering and the development of Fort Leonard Wood.

The idea for a museum began in 1960 with the donation of several items belonging to General Wood. The mementos, which had been displayed at various points around the post, found a permanent home in 1971. In 1988, the facility was re-designated as the U.S. Army Engineer Museum.

The facility is really two museums under one title. One, the new brick structure, features the accomplishments and history of military engineering. The other, across the street, is comprised of twelve World War II-era buildings, restored to their appearance during that war's mobilization and training at Fort Leonard Wood.

The Engineer Museum houses 12,000 artifacts, about fifteen percent of which are on display at any one time. Veterans, like visitor Walter Kline, who offered to send personal slides of Korea to the museum, have donated many items. "They are getting up there in years now," explained Russ of veterans. "They look at the foot locker in the basement and think, 'Why don't I take this to a museum?'"

Other items are borrowed from other museums or can be obtained from the Center of Military History in Anniston Depot, Alabama. "Our objective as curators is to preserve any object in our care for as long as possible," said Russ. "Anything man-made will eventually self-destruct. Our job is to protect items from light, heat, humidity, and dirt."

The history of military engineering dates back to ancient days of battering rams, catapults, and sieges. Some items displayed are just about as old as war itself. Russ' personal favorite is a signet ring belonging to Lysimachus, a Greek military engineer who served Alexander the Great.

"An American engineer working for the Greek government found it. He wasn't sure who it represented. It was studied by Hellenic and Smithsonian experts who authenticated it."

To find the museum, take the Fort's I-44 exit and enter the post at the Main Gate on Missouri

Displays in the museum spill out onto the floor like rubble.

Avenue. Missouri Avenue eventually becomes Constitution Avenue. Proceed to South Dakota Avenue and turn left. The museum is located two blocks on the left. You can telephone (573-596-0780).

The museum is open Monday through Saturday from 10 a.m. to 4 p.m. and is closed Sundays and all holidays.

The Big Award

Ragtag Horse Jumps over Competition

For odd horse out, Doc's Repeat hasn't done so badly. Overshadowed by his stable mates, dogged by his past, his career has almost been an afterthought in owner Bob Swick's scrapbook of accomplishments.

"He and Pat (Dunham) just clicked," says Bob Swick. "Her working Doc is something you just have to watch."

Yet saddled with Lady Luck, Doc's Repeat, in 1997, quietly gave Swick a lot to smile about. That February the frosted sorrel earned Supreme Champion Appaloosa status, previously held by only ten other horses so distinguished in the Association's fifty-year history. For good measure, he earned five High Point in the Nation medallions in Hunter Hack, Open Jumping, Working Hunter, Lady Side Saddle, and Senior Saddle Seat Pleasure.

Given his background and training, Doc shouldn't have earned one pewter medallion. He has no pedigree papers. He is ridden by his part-time trainer. He works out in a clearing behind Swick's Lebanon, Missouri, farm. He trains over makeshift jumps concocted of industrial barrels and fence posts.

Credit the roll of the dice for Doc's full shelf in the trophy case. His uncommon athletic ability was only accidentally discovered, and his devotion for trainer/rider, Pat Dunham, unintentionally developed. "It was just luck to find the horses I have," said Swick. "People spend a lot more money than me and never get as far. It was luck having Pat come along when she did. And, there was just the luck of timing."

Doc was never purchased for the show circuit. Searching for trail horses in 1991, Swick bought the horse because of his look-alike sister and the free-flowing way he moved. Doc was an undistinguished entity in the small entourage of animals that milled around Swick as he walked to the barn. When Swick's friends saddled for an afternoon ride in the Ozarks, Doc was chosen only after the other horses were taken. He had no bright career or encouraging future expectations that would excuse him bucking off his rider on the Chief Joseph Trail Ride. It wasn't long after that when the horse tossed off an inexperienced rider and broke her arm.

Naturally, Swick was not inclined to fool with the horse any more.

"We first thought he was ornery, a rogue," Swick recalled of his then four-year-old gelding. "I was ready to ship him for dog food because of his temper. I'm just glad Pat decided to try her hand at him."

Pat Dunham was a part-time rider for the Gasconade School of Riding where Swick often dropped by. In a last ditch effort to save the horse from a career in a can, Dunham suggested jumping him.

"From the moment she got on him, he's never shown another ill moment," Swick admitted. "He and Pat just clicked. Her working Doc is something you just have to watch. She's firm, and at the same time, loving. He responds to her not out of fear of punishment, but a desire to please."

"I didn't even try him over a training jump," recalled Dunham. "I showed him a little eighteen-inch jump. He didn't try to step over it. He met it nice and square. I could tell he liked jumping. We just found out what he enjoyed doing. Once we knew he could jump, we just had to work on speed so he could handle the corners."

Dunham agreed to ride Doc and then, unhappy with his conditioning, began training him for his newfound destiny herself. It was a long-distance arrangement for everyone. With Doc quartered back at Swick's Lebanon farm, Swick circled the sixty-mile round trip from his principal's duties at Fort Leonard Wood's middle school. Dunham drove her own fifty-mile loop from her stitcher job at Richland's H.D. Lee plant. She squeezed Doc's training time between her day job, the weather, and her responsibilities toward Swick's other Appaloosa competitors, Pac Man and Willie. As either rider or trainer, she showed up four times a week, alternating workouts among the trio. The sixty-minute routine included trotting poles, cavaletting, small jumps, and other gymnastic activities. It didn't end until after cool downs, feeding, bathing, and clipping back at the barn.

"I felt sorry for the horses," Dunham said. "My guys never got any petting or playing time. Whenever I showed up, they knew they were going to get worked."

Training facilities on Swick's one hundred forty-acre farm requires winding through the blackjack and cedars behind his barn. The pasture beyond the frog pond slopes into the buck brush and lamb's quarter. There, Dunham concocted the practice jumps herself, using industrial barrels, tires, and two by six boards.

"In the beginning, it was a trial-and-error process for everyone," said Dunham. "You watch and learn, read a lot, and go to clinics."

"Working Doc in an open-air practice area keeps the Appaloosa clear-minded after his seven show years," said Swick, "He can jump over logs in the woods. His mind is not arena locked but rider associated."

Dunham said, "A lot of horses only know the horse show life. They don't even know what a fence is or how to respect it. They've never been out on their own or in a herd environment. On the other hand, I have total faith that the most inexperienced rider could go across country tomorrow on Doc. He wouldn't shy at every little thing. He wouldn't trip over his feet. He could take care of himself, and he would take good care of his rider."

Away from the competition training, Doc joins Swick's herd of a dozen Appaloosa and Paints. Monty and Tex,

Swick's own Chief Joseph mounts, rule the equine hierarchy; Doc ranks further down the social order, buddying with Willie, his show comrade.

Swick's do-it-ourselves operation has resulted in a close knit bond between the trio. "We don't have just a trainer-

"At first we thought he was ornery, a rogue," says Bob Swick.

rider-owner-horse relationship," Swick explained. "We're like family. We've been together nine years. We've got one of the longest love-hate relationships of any non-married couple I know," he said. "But we're an example that it doesn't matter whether you're a one-horse outfit or not. If you get the right combination of horse and rider, you can accomplish the same as people with a lot of money and a lot of horses."

Swick unfailingly credits Doc's transformation to Dunham. "He's a natural athlete and totally willing to coop-erate," said Swick. "Their ability to communicate and understand each other is the secret."

Dunham shys away from any mystical bond analysis. "He's not the prettiest or the smartest horse, but when you put a task before him, he'll try to do it," she said. "He's turned into a really laid back, a family-type of animal now. He really tries to do anything you ask. It's just a matter of basics and letting him get used to what you want from him."

Doc's first experience as Hunter Jumper followed a scant four weeks after his initial look at a fence. In his first schooling show, he placed in the top five in his class. Under Dunham's tutelage, Doc led the nation in Working Hunter and Second Year Green Hunter two seasons later.

Still, Doc remained understudy to the bigger stars in the corral. Swick was more attached to Pac Man, his mount in Keyhole and Figure Eight classes. And Willie, whom Dunham had broken from lead, was her favorite. In 1993, the troupe hit the competition circuit hard, chasing points for Willie to finish as High Point Year End Preliminary Jumper, World Champion Preliminary Jumper, and Reserve World Champion Second Year Green Hunter. Swick's eight-second races on Pac Man earned him a silver belt buckle in Keyhole and Figure Eight. Doc brought up the rear with Year End High Point, Second Year Green Hunter, and Year End High Point Working Hunter honors.

Their seven-medallion year exacted a price. Though they cut expenses by bunking in the trailer, borrowing equipment, and making costumes, twenty-six weekends on the road depleted Swick's pocketbook and Dunham's emotional reserves. Pac Man was sold. Willie sustained an injury. Except for Reserve World Champion Preliminary Jumper and High Point Preliminary Jumper distinctions, Doc did little more than neigh and nicker in the woods.   "Having a $13,000 hobby was stressful for an educator's salary, and Pat wanted to pursue other things," said Swick of their hiatus.

Doc's moment arrived in 1996. Working just one Appaloosa, Dunham had time to concentrate on the horse's personality and innate abilities. "He has a real laid-back personality and a dry sense of humor," said Dunham. "That has to do with training, doing something over and over. He's experienced and has seen a lot over the years. Nothing's a big deal to him anymore."

Dunham began expanding his program, adding Side Saddle and Saddle Seat Pleasure to challenge his workouts. She threw in Trail purely for recreation. "Doc's attitude is always work, work, work," said Dunham. "He may not execute something perfectly, but he is always more than willing to please. He will try his best for his rider."

More importantly, Dunham and Swick realized that throughout his career Doc routinely finished with seventy percent of the points he was eligible to earn. In the process, he had acquired the necessary ROMs for Superior Working Hunter, Versatility status, and Appaloosa Club Champion. The hundred-point requirement for Supreme Appaloosa Champion seemed within reach by the summer of 1997.

"Until then, we were competing just for fun," said Swick. "Then, at mid-season, we noticed besides doing well in Side Saddle and Saddle Seat Pleasure, Doc had a chance to get in the national point race for Hunter Hack, Open Jumping, and Working Hunter. If we were that close without really trying hard, we decided to see how far he could go if we put our minds to it again."

The duo topped off the gas tank to garner the requisite

Dunham shys away from any mystical bond analysis. "He's not the prettiest or the smartest horse, but when you put a task before him, he'll try to do it," she says.

points. Leaving Missouri's eight regional shows, they traveled from Texas to Florida and Oklahoma to Illinois in a seventeen weekend blitz between July and November. Besides his Supreme Appaloosa certificate, by season's end, Doc had earned High Point in the Nation medallions in five classes: Hunter Hack, Open Jumping, Working Hunter, Lady Side Saddle, and Senior Saddle Seat Pleasure. His nearest competitors finished twelve to eight points behind him.

"It is very rare for one horse to succeed in such a wide range of classes," said Swick. "Today's specialty horse is either a jumper or a pleasure or a halter horse. That Doc led the nation in five different classes definitely shows his versatility."

Rather than retire the thirteen-year-old completely, Swick and Dunham have moved him into new categories. Six-year-old Bobby Gonzales is training with Doc in the walk-trot English equitation class, and Swick is looking at a doctor's buggy to use in buckboard driving.

"I've accomplished everything I ever dreamed about being an Appaloosa owner," said Swick. "Once I got the 1994 medallions, I dreamed of a Versatility Champion. Doc made that a reality. With Pat's effort and Doc's ability, he has become a Supreme Appaloosa Champion. He has fulfilled my dreams beyond my wildest expectations."

Life's bridesmaids, stand-ins, sidekicks, and also-rans sometimes get lost in the crowd, but in one Cinderella year, Doc's Repeat stepped center ring all by himself. Once just a tag-a-long horse, he doesn't stand behind anything any more.

The Big Test

Wilderness Exploration Project

Students in the Wilderness Exploration Project go to school where walls are made of oak and hickory bark; the ceiling is a canopy of branches. Corridors are boot wide and visible only by the mash of pine needles. They forget Saturday cartoons, buckle into backpacks half as tall as their height, and head toward lessons in success.

Wood Middle School librarian, Steve Kirkbride, points to landmarks for the sixth graders who have hiked to the top of the Paddy Creek Wilderness Area overhang.

With their teacher-guides, these middle school students,

working as a team, will encounter new adventures. In hiking shoes, on mule back, setting up camp, or paddling a canoe, a dozen high-risk children at Wood Middle School at Fort Leonard Wood will be too busy to remember past failures and frustrations. Each task, a minuscule triumph on the trail, is one step toward building their self-esteem.

Wilderness Exploration Project weekends target children with low self-esteem. Such as Allison who describes herself as "dumb" and "stupid" and then validates her verbal comments with failing grades, and John, an uncertain child who wants to do his best but isn't sure his best is worth doing. And there is Andy, who likes to do what is expected of him but is so overwhelmed by the enormity of the task that he ricochets into trouble like a balloon that's lost its knot.

These students are ill suited for traditional schoolroom atmospheres. They don't qualify for special behavior disorders or learning disability classes which provide one-on-one help. In the regular classroom, they neither succeed nor fail. Every assignment is an overwhelming struggle.

Created in 1994, WEP embraces these at-risk kids. Larry Cloninger, then a counselor at Wood Middle School, outlined an outdoor program designed for overcoming unfamiliar, if not formidable obstacles. The message to participants is subliminal. If you can navigate a canoe, build a campsite, purify water, or ride a mule, what's the big deal about mixed fractions or subordinate clauses?

WEP's concept met with administrative approval. "I truly believe in the project," said Bob Swick, Wood Middle School principal. "If we save or help just one kid, it would be worth the time and effort."

With the school district approval, Cloninger and Swick

applied for a Department of Elementary and Secondary Education Incentive Grant in 1994. Its $18,000, along with the school district's additional money, bought tents, sleeping bags, canoes, life jackets, cooking equipment, hiking shoes, rain gear, cold-weather clothing, and food. It also financed training and salaries for staff. A continuation grant in 1995 replenished supplies and bankrolled building a canoe trailer and storage facilities.

A year-long project, WEP begins in September when the entire faculty recommends about seventy students for consideration. These sixth, seventh, and eighth graders take the Piers-Harris Children's Self-Concept Scale, a self-esteem inventory test. Those with the greatest needs are individually interviewed. Students are placed in three-person, same-sex teams. Their outings, since the first year, have been coed. Team coordinator Steve Kirkbride said, "Instead of taking all boys and then all girls, we thought it would be helpful for the guys to see that the girls are capable of doing anything they do."

Students quickly realize a WEP adventure is no casual walk in the woods. Before they step over a log, they are well aware of the expectations and practice them. In early fall, orientation includes first aid procedures and assembling equipment. In the library, they practice pitching tents and packing sleeping bags, cooking gear, water-purifying paraphernalia, tents, and food in their backpacks.

Like Allison, who had only camped in her grandparent's backyard, most students have little hiking/camping experience. Conquering each preparation task, each challenge they incur in the Wilderness is an opportunity for students to build self-esteem. Paddy Creek Wilderness, thirty miles from the school, has a myriad of challenges to conquer. The trail heads slightly upward through a mixture of hardwood trees, short leaf pine, and oaks. Students must walk to the campsite, about a two-mile hike, where they pick their way around outcroppings and are instructed to keep away from the steep cliffs. Angie admitted, "The backpacking is hard. At first it isn't; then the pack gets heavy."

Getting to the top is worth all the expended effort for the students. Paul wrote in his journal: *Saturday's trail hike really gave me the opportunity to experience nature. It was a good experience that a lot of kids don't ever get to see.*

After each WEP outing, students track their feelings in a journal. They are unflinchingly honest critiquing the activity and their own anxieties.

Tommy wrote: *Last Saturday was a day I will probably will never forget. I went on a wilderness trail. At first, I was nervous, because I thought everyone might have the same clothes as I had...When I got there I was surprised to see that I look different.*

...We checked each other's packs and headed on the trail. Some of the team had got behind so we waited for them. Then, we rested to eat lunch on a cliff where we had a perfect view of the river. I had a wonderful time.

Past the crest of the ridge and the overhang above Paddy Creek, the group threads toward the campsite. Climbing the rocky terrain carrying a twenty-five pound backpack is a physical strain, especially on the smaller eighty-five pound kids. Expending extraordinary energy en route, kids drink a lot of water. It is critical that they purify the water in Paddy Creek so they will have enough for cooking two meals and replenishing the bottled water they have consumed. Leaving backpacks at the campsite, they walk down a winding path

300 feet to the creek valley and then return in a hard thirty-minute climb back up the ridge.

Setting up camp provides a bag full of accomplishments. Selecting a level place for the tent and getting all the poles

Students pack tents, sleeping bags, cooking utensils, purification equipment, food, and water into the wilderness for an overnight campout.

in the right places require team work students rarely use in school. They must prepare supper from packages of dehydrated beef stew and noodles stroganoff and clean their own utensils. The "You-Dig-It" bathroom facilities are a new experience for all of them. Ashley wrote: *The WEP trip was fun, but the only part I didn't like was using the bathroom outside. And when are we going to spend the night again?*

Paddy Creek area is also used for the mule trail ride. This challenge experience was added to the program the second year. Orientation to riding fundamentals and getting acquainted with Pat and Sadie and Dynamite takes place at Jim Robertson's corral in Belle. A week later, students saddle up their mules for a six-hour day trip in the wilderness.

Tammy wrote in her journal: *We rode mules. It was fun. I bruised my muscle. But I still want to go again. A little bruise won't stop me. I think this is a good way to get rid of stress.*

The spring/summer WEP activities include a seven-mile bike ride on the Katy Trail and float trips down the Little Piney River. Students watch videos on canoe strokes and water safety in orientation. When the weather is quiet and the river's water levels are stable, the group pushes off into a daylong or overnight float. One student rides between two counselors, dividing time paddling between front, middle, and back positions. The adventure always includes a pull up to a sandbar so students can swim, snorkel, or hunt crawdads along the bank. The experiences maneuvering a canoe successfully down the river, around the submerged logs, through shallow water, and over small riffles are confidence builders.

Before school ends, students are given the self-esteem test again to measure numerically how they view themselves. Their progress is charted. All students have showed measurable gains, progressing as many as fifty points up the scale of self-esteem.

The change in Allison demonstrates the program's success better than tests or graphs. Prior to her inclusion into WEP, she seemed headed for another year of academic failure and perhaps repeating the seventh grade. "I didn't feel good about myself," she recalled. "I used to think I couldn't do things like my school work. I thought I was going to flunk. I was getting F's in almost all my classes. But, not any more. Because I saw that I could do stuff on trips, I knew I could do other things. My schoolwork is better this year." Her grades improved at least a letter grade in all her subjects.

Allison was invited to return a second year in the WEP project to be a student leader. Her job was to assist new members as they prepared for upcoming outings or to answer questions while on the trail.

"Allison went from a quiet kid with a negative cloud around her to a vibrant student," observed Swick. "She reflects a much more positive attitude about herself. There is a light about her now." What better success rate can a program provide than this?

Because students consume so much water on the long hike to the camp site, their first task is to purify and replenish their water supply.

Herbs Make Scents to Her

Ethel Hickey

"Whether it's a weed or a herb depends on your state of mind," said Ethel Hickey. The self-styled medicine woman, and Steelville, Missouri resident, views medicinal plants as the Tylenol of the past.

Like early Ozarkers, Ethel Hickey uses a backyard herb garden for relief from life's aches and pains.

More than a first-aid kit, the great Ozark outdoors is Ethel's passion, vocation, and inspiration. She and her husband, Pat, are rooted in the terrain. The researcher, botanist, teacher, ecologist, and artist draws sustenance from the plants surrounding her log cabin home.

"Modern medicines—like aspirin and ibuprofen—just disguise symptoms until the body eventually overcomes the ailment," said the longtime instructor of Elderhostel courses. "They don't pay attention to the cause of a headache. But a medicinal tea, with the properly chosen root, leaf, or seed, targets the ailment itself."

The plants outside the fence row were, after all, just about all pioneer Ozarkers had. Raspberry leaf was their Band-Aid; Milkweed removed warts. Skullcap tranquilized; puccoon sterilized. Sassafras cleansed the liver; sumac pulled moisture from the body. Like her predecessors, Ethel includes herbs with her fruit trees, grapevines, and vegetable garden. Down the winding path from their cabin, she grows yellow dock to purify the blood, lobelia for her asthma, and pennyroyal to repel fleas in her dogs' beds. "They're all part of every good thing that you need," she said.

Hickey believes concern over nature's medicine cabinet was, in part, responsible for the distance maintained between Ozark neighbors. "People didn't like folks living too close. Everyone would be using the same herb patch. A lot of plants were used for a variety of ailments, and a whole variety of ailments could be treated with a single plant. It was a concern about supply."

Who'd share blue flag when it relieved earache as a poultice and vomiting as a tea? Divvy up chickweed? Swallowed, it was a laxative; as a salve it helped skin infections. Ration Virginia snakeroot? It cured snakebite and putrid sores. Dole out buckleweed and buckthorn? One stopped diarrhea, and the other ended constipation. Blackberry tea toned and tightened the skin as well as encouraged pregnancy.

"Women drank it to tone the uterus and later condition muscles for an easier delivery," said Hickey. "In a complicated delivery, it helped extract afterbirth. Black cohash and pennyroyal, steeped as a tea, prevented cell growth. They regulated the menstrual cycle and were abortive if taken too much or often."

"The spring tonic was a fun one," she said. "After a winter of limited activities and limited nutrition, early Ozarkers believed in purging. The tonic stimulated circulation, the liver, and kidneys. In a day or two, it'd clean out your intestines, make you vomit, get you breathing fast, and make your sinuses run. It cleansed your entire body."

Though helpful with either gender's aches and bruises, herb uses seemed suited for women concerns—birth control, female trouble, cosmetics, salves, and lotions,

"Men were supposed to be tough," said Ethel. "They didn't admit to taking anything, except maybe moonshine."

Ethel believes doctoring the family was a natural for the woman. Mama knew what her children ate, where they played, what animals were around, and what lurked beyond the chicken house or in it. Instead of sending for a physician, a virtual stranger, many depended on Dr. Mom's eagle eye and intuition.

Ethel, dressed in a handwoven, handmade dress, lectures at Potosi's YMCA of the Ozarks. She explains a hundred common plants used on the Plateau, but encourages students to read and research on their own. At home, she takes advantage of the plant's medicinal benefits.

"I use a lot of herbs," she said. "I just went to the doctor for the first time in ten years. She said to come back when I got sick. I believe herbs help maintain good health."

To control her asthma, Ethel takes a daily tonic, made with a vinegar base and culinary herbs that strengthen the respiratory system. Still, she admitted, "If I had a huge attack, I'd use my inhaler. If that didn't work, I'm on the way to hospital."

While investigating growth of the running buffalo clover for Missouri's Department of Conservation, she cut her hand badly with a scythe. "I was thirty minutes from the car, so I wrapped it in a raspberry leaf. By the time I got to a Band-Aid, it was sealed. Three days later it was gone."

When Pat stumbled into stinging nettles, Ethel spread jewelweed juice on his legs. "It's a preventative," explained Ethel. "It coats the skin and keeps the poison ivy from reacting with the body's protein."

Ethel's expertise in medicinal plants grew from an interest in edible plants. "When I first moved here, I had that Ozark spirit of 'Make do with what you had,'" said Ethel. "I started studying wild edible plants. When I researched them to avoid anything poisonous, I would read warnings about times when a plant was good for medicine but not for food. Poke greens, for example, are good to eat at certain times and at others are used as medicine."

Her interest in herbs grew to workshop-size courses for area schools. It grafted easily to the couple's close-to-the-land lifestyle. She and Pat have enlarged an abandoned hunting cabin into a 3200-foot sanctuary for their artistic and botanist interests. Fourteen miles outside of Steelville, it is a work-in-progress. They hand peeled 950 logs for its two stories. With a master's degree in ceramics and sculpture, Ethel displays oil paintings and bronze castings in their Great Room. Dried bouquets of beggar's lice, smartweed, and goldenrod are vased around the room.

"For a while I was enamored with the post-Civil War Ozarks, like the 1850s," Ethel said. "But I was much younger when we started. The older I get, the more conveniences I want."

The Hickeys combine the new and the old. Their television and VCR are out of sight, hidden under the stairs, but her computer merits its own office overlooking the forest. The water only appears to run from a hand pump. Its plumbing is camouflaged under the sink. All the walls and floors are pine, and Ethel cooks with wood. Pat's grandfather's double barrel shotgun hangs over the walnut mantle. "It was my grandmother's wedding gift to my grandfather," said Pat. "Traditionally it symbolized the male being the provider of the family."

Daily, Pat drives a one hundred eighty-eight mile round trip to his St. Louis County job. He leaves at 4 a.m. on Interstate 44 and is home soon enough to squirrel hunt or fish if he wants. Meantime, Ethel's other career has taken root in the Ozark forest.

A transplant from the suburbs, Ethel once taught gymnastics in St. Louis County and then founded a summer girls camp near Steelville. Relocating in the eastern Ozarks, she taught art fourteen years in Steelville's school system and then returned to St. Louis for an art career.

"Nature was my second love," she recalled. She studied plant ecology, taught in Missouri universities, and then worked with Missouri's Department of Conservation as an assistant botanist.

Through nearly half of Missouri counties, she tracked

four federally endangered species. The stacks of historic records, geology maps, and aerial photos were as tangled as the landscape she tramped around, locating surviving plants or potential relocation sites.

She believes her efforts rescued running buffalo clover. Once spread by buffalo herds as they moved between St. Louis and Springfield, the native plant was thought nearly extinct. Largely due to her four-year reintroduction of it in the Mark Twain National Forest, it is scheduled to be upgraded to "threatened species."

"I would be pleased if I were responsible for keeping a species from becoming extinct on this planet," she said. Though the project's funding was cut, she continues to voluntarily monitor the clover.

When not involved with the house renovation or conservation causes, Ethel teaches her Elderhostel courses. Besides Potosi's YMCA of the Ozarks, she conducts workshops at Wren Lake and Mt. Vernon, Illinois, at Rolla Technical Institute, and Mineral Area College in Park Hills. Her subjects includes leaf identification, wildflowers, aromatherapy, and medicinal herbs. Her newest courses, "Landscaping, a Personal Space" and "Black Pearls of the Ozarks," are earthbound too.

"People have known for years herbal medicines work, but they didn't have the clinical research, under strong controls, for the medical community to back it," said Ethel. "Now many are accepted because more research is being done."

The rest of the world may just be catching up to Ethel Hickey. She's way ahead of those now realizing remedies of the past have value for the present.

Finger-Snapping Music

Jim Widner's Big Band Sound

"**I**f you don't snap your fingers, I'm doing something wrong," said Jim Widner. Listening to the Jefferson City resident is never a stationary experience. For three decades, Widner has been sending music from his hands to his audience's.

Under the trumpet's lip-splitters, the saxophone's mournful lament, and the piano's mischievous scamper, he leans over his four-string bass and digs in. With the flur-

"This bass is more famous than I am," says Jim Widner of his 350-year-old instrument. On it, his fingers do the talking

ry of a million notes, in the drive of a hundred rhythms, Jim Widner telegraphs his passion—jazz. "Once I feel the chemistry between the bass and the drummer, I don't have to do anything else," said Widner. "I could play all night."

Sometimes he has. From California to Florida, Widner, on his own, and with his twenty-member band, performs on stage and teaches in the classroom. The Jim Widner Big Band's CDs merited Grammy consideration and earned national acclaim. It's an unusual dialect for a man born and raised in bluegrass music territory.

"Country is popular, but it's not the avenue I chose to go," admitted Widner. "I just had to work harder to get to the places where jazz was strong and flourished."

Widner's destiny did not come easy. Just getting to the music stand required some doing. His mother, a single parent, couldn't even afford the rent on a school instrument, so he volunteered to play cello in the stringed orchestra.

"It didn't take very long to realize I wasn't good at that," he recalled, "But I wanted to get in the band program."

Fortunately, his band director offered an instrument Widner could stand behind. Though he traded the cello for the concert bass, he had yet to find his calling. That needed a song.

"During a high school assembly, the band was all dressed up in white jackets, and the spotlights were on. Then it played 'Peter Gunn.' That was the first time I had heard jazz played. Right then and there I said, 'I'm going to play bass in that band.'"

And he did. Possessed of an instrument and a music style, Widner still lacked an inspiration until he attended a Stan Kenton concert.

"The power of his band was mind boggling," he said. His director urged him to approach John Worster, Kenton's bass player after the concert. Widner, a shy teenager, hung back.

"I was terrified," recalled Widner, "but he saw me and said, 'I'll be looking for you at camp.'"

With that small encouragement and a scholarship, Widner headed to Kenton's summer camp. During the day, he studied with the big band legends and at night attended their concerts.

"I would stand in the wings, watching the rhythm section. I just had to be near it," he said.

When Kenton moved his "Jazz Orchestra in Residence" programs from Indiana to California, Widner followed on a Greyhound bus. In four summers, Widner was playing on stage with Kenton and teaching with him in California, New York, and Maryland. Widner even initiated Kenton's Midwest return.

"I told him I was running a babysitting service, bringing twenty-five Missouri kids with me," said Widner. When he approached Springfield's (Missouri) Drury College, its camp became a second Ozark home for the big band sound.

Between camps, Widner toured with Kenton, the Glen Miller Orchestra, and Buddy DeFranco. He picked up an undergraduate degree from the University of Missouri, a master's degree from Memphis State University, and worked on postgraduate courses while attending the University of North Texas. His teaching experiences have been many—North Texas State University, Memphis State University, and Southwest Missouri State University in Springfield. When his mentor died in 1979, the Kenton program died with him.

"I waited nine years for someone to pick up the jazz education scene," recalled Widner. "No one ever did. I had to do something about it. Missouri had been such a hot bed of jazz education. I got enough people to accept my crazy dream. I took a financial bath for a couple years, but I believed in it. I had to try."

To resurrect the summer camp concept, Widner needed a band that could work with student musicians and then demonstrate how the technical talk transcends dissection. Gathering friends from his touring days, the Jim Widner Big Band was born. Their collective resume reads like a jazz hall of fame: Kenton, Woody Herman, Buddy Rich, Count Basie, Louis Bellson, and Doc Severinson.

"It has some of the greatest jazz players in the world—that's a given," said Widner. "But I want them because they are great teachers."

Jazz education marks Widner's philosophy like bars on a staff. In early spring, the Big Band's tour combines performance with instruction. Widner invariably schedules student clinics after every performance. The trombones and trumpets scatter through the school or auditorium to work one-on-one with aspiring artists. With young bass players looking on, Widner demonstrates how the snap of the hand enlivens the beat. He tells them drummer John "the Baron" Von Ohlen's edict, "If you're bored playing time, you haven't found it yet."

Widner's summers crisscross the country. Beginning with their decade-old big band camp at Drury College, Widner and crew show and tell their expertise to 500 students in Nevada, Texas, Alabama, and Missouri. By day, band members conduct master classes, teach theory, and rehearse with student bands.

"They can both play and teach," said sax player, Maria

Navd. "A lot of people have natural talent, but don't know how to explain anything." A second-year band camper, she and four others received scholarships from the Hot Springs, Arkansas Jazz Society. Mindful of the financial struggles of his youth, Widner unfailingly provides financial aid for students.

Their twelve-hour day climaxes with an evening concert. Kids who once were inexperienced with jazz's fixed arrangement style and improvisational skills instantly respond to the obvious: the whole is more than the sum of its parts. They recognize technique—the chord variations, the overlay of scales, the trombone smears, but their whistles and ovations tribute the fire and smoke of their mentors' music. Student interest, in fact, sparked Widner's two CDs. "Students kept asking for recordings," said Widner. "We thought we'd better get to a studio and see what we could come out with."

The band recorded 1995's "Yesterdays and Today" and 1996's "Body and Soul" after finishing their teaching and performing responsibilities in Springfield, Missouri. Jazz experts recognize legendary Bill Perkins on tenor sax and hints of the Band's collective credentials, but their trademark starts with Jim Widner's bass. "This band has a hard swinging, powerful sound," Widner said. "The drive comes from the rhythm section."

Each recording climbed on the national charts and joined Grammy balloting consideration with notables such as Dave Grusin, Bill Holman Band, and the Lincoln Center Jazz Band.

"For a poor kid from Lebanon, Missouri, just being on the same sheet with them is pretty good company," Widner admitted.

Though Widner has toured four continents and pinned appearance locations into forty-nine states on his office map, he is firmly grounded in the Ozarks. Loyal to his roots, he and his Big Band regularly return to his hometown, donating their concerts to benefit its music program.

Beyond performing for a president and playing in a sports stadium full of jazz fans, Widner confesses his career's shining moment included his children.

"Lance played drums, and I played bass while Jamie danced," he recalled of his daughter's senior dance recital. "That had to have been the highlight of my career."

Jim Widner is a quiet man. He and his bass stand at the edge of his ensemble, just beyond the bright lights. Never demanding, they speak with the unmistakable jazz beat. With a lifelong passion for a unique musical vocabulary, Jim Widner lets his fingers do the talking.

"Hopefully, I've made a difference to my kids and the students I've worked with for thirty years. They don't have to become career jazz musicians, but if they appreciate and understand this language a little more, I've done something right."

Across Our Wide Missouri
Bob Priddy

No other tone nor tenor, cadence, or rhythm tolls for the Show-Me State like Bob Priddy's. Consummate storyteller, historian, and journalist, Priddy has spun a career on retelling the past and reporting the present for Missouri radio. Since 1982 radio listeners have eaten their breakfasts, scheduled their showers, and driven to work by the clockwork schedule of his "Across Our Wide Missouri."

Priddy's five minute stories capture tiny history lessons of the common man as well as the famous who helped create the images that represent the Show-Me state. With an ear cocked toward the unusual and an eye toward the past, he has

Radio journalist, Bob Priddy, has filled three books with verbal snapshots of the famous and obscure, the trivial and monumental in the Show-Me State. (Photo courtesy of Bob Priddy.)

discovered the unique and the significant about the people who have walked across the pages of Missouri history.

He discovers the first speed limit (9 mph in Mexico, Missouri), the first car, and the first flag. He explains why artist George Caleb Bingham was bald and that Peyton Hayden wore his hair braided like a China man. He tells of John G. Neihardt's part in bringing Methodism to Missouri and David Rice Atchinson's brush with glory as President of the United States for a day. He spins tales of flat boat operators, soldiers, politicians, governors, inventors, and scalliwags.

"There's never been anything like 'Across Our Wide Missouri' in broadcasting," Priddy said. "And I don't know of very many things in other states. There's been series of programs but not a daily thing on radio or television."

Priddy's personal love affair with Missouri began thirty-five years ago when he left the cornfields of Illinois to enroll in Journalism School at the University of Missouri in Columbia. Since then he has been living, reporting, and researching in his adopted state. Although originally headed for a career in newspaper writing, when his unusual voice was noticed, his career turned to the microphone.

Missouri as a whole began to benefit from Priddy's talents while he worked at KLIK radio in Jefferson City. During the 1971 Celebration of the Missouri Sesquicentennial, Priddy referred to Floyd Shoemaker's book, *Missouri Day by Day* in a series of sketches about Missouri history. "I used his book as a basis for starting my program. I used his dates and material if he mentioned a specific event or person and then did my own research. He did nothing with crime other than Jesse James or sports. Sports is an important part of any individual," said Priddy.

Before long, Priddy created his own formula—one that tells a story commemorating each day of the year. His idea was simple—make it short, make it sweet, and make it about the people or events that thread the fabric of the past.

First called, "Missouri Day by Day," Priddy's program aired for four years. In 1975, when he moved to the MissouriNet, he took the program with him, renaming it "Across Our Wide Missouri." To keep the program alive, Priddy sandwiched in research between his duties as news director and reporter of current events at the Capitol. His research was not obscure. He found the subjects for the program in the daily obituaries, at the state historical society, in the indexes of nonfiction books, and in more than 300 other easily accessible sources.

In the early eighties, Priddy hit upon the idea to put his "Across Our Wide" *Missouri* on the printed page. "Publishers said, 'We don't really think this day-by-day thing will work. Put it in chronological order.' I said, 'Everybody does that. People are bored stiff with that.'" He eventually won his point and *Across Our Wide Missouri*, the book, remained true to his radio format.

When Priddy wrote his manuscript, he did not have the benefit of the present-day computer delete button or a laser printer. To write, he retreated into a trailer during his vacation time. Clanking out his stories on an old Royal typewriter, Priddy wrote a six hundred eighty page manuscript in two weeks. He soon discovered writing on paper was immensely different from scripting a story for radio. On the advice of his editor, he returned to the typewriter and cut the manuscript to five hundred pages.

What resulted was Volume I of *Across Our Wide Missouri,* which chronicles the 180 days between January and June. Volume II that followed in 1984 finished the calendar year. Over the years, the books have sold several thousand copies.

"I'm told for regional books, that's pretty good," Priddy said. He then smilingly revealed that the books have financed a college education for his two children, Elizabeth and Robert.

There are problems with the books, though. It is difficult to find a particular subject without thumbing through the entire year. However, readers and listeners were bound to the day-by-day format until Priddy's third book, *Across Our Wide Missouri Volume III* remedied the needle-in-the-haystack-of-history search by providing an index. The index lists by battle, city, and person the historical events from all three books.

Priddy has yet to capture in verbal or written word all he wants to say about Missouri. His cluttered desk at the Missouri Net office contains file boxes of ideas and possible story ideas. Each five-minute story takes eight hours or more to develop, and his duties on the air and in Senate chambers consume much of his day.

Besides being historian, Priddy's prime occupation remains in the present and the telling of ongoing news. He arrives at the MissouriNet's offices at 5:00 a.m. and tapes his "Across Our Wide Missouri" show for the day and writes the four or five stories that will air on the hour and half hour from the MissouriNet. Once the show is taped, Priddy heads for the Capitol where he prowls chambers and attends committee meetings to report on legislative and executive events for the seventy-one stations the MissouriNet serves.

Priddy often ventures from the newsroom and the

library to speak about his favorite topic to his preferred audience, school children. "Everyone of us is tied to an historical event," he said. "I pull out the book, and it's something they can relate to. When somebody famous was born or died on their birthday, then history becomes more fun."

Feeling obligated to personally fulfill his newsroom duties, Priddy seldom ventures far from home. While daily living his role, Priddy comfortably wears a coat of past memories and present events. "I don't think you can be a good journalist if you aren't something of a historian. You can't tell people what's going on without telling the context of the events. The public is not served with a surface description of the event. *Across Our Wide Missouri* has helped people understand what our state has evolved with what is."

Epilogue

hat my eye recognized and my words recorded across this region, my heart had not yet embraced. Like oracle of ancient times and reporter in this, I looked into the cosmos just to tell a story.

I had to leave the Ozarks to learn I loved it, for I believed vivid, majestic scenery of far-off locations and philosophical

The Ozark hills rise and fall like long, slow, deep breaths. Their rhythm rests and calms the heart.

conversations would better feed my soul. I gladly left the rocky soil, stretching like rusty skin over the hills. I turned my face from broad-leafed scrub oak as it fanned the heat of summer sun. Ordinary talk of common folk chipped like cavern chirt against my hard ambitions. Thus, I drove my car, with ignorance packed tightly in its trunk, beyond the scent of blue-seed cedars and off the Plateau where I had lived.

The Kansas Plains gave me pause. Outside the car window, its harvest halved the world at the horizon. Abutted to the sapphire sky, uncut wheat glistened gold, like burnished strands brushed a hundred times by fair-haired heroines. Harvesting the ripened grain, hand-sized combines, moved by tiny specks of men, left black parts behind them. The shafts, scalped of their topaz, fell tow headed by the acre. Sun-fed, this amber landscape spread into spaces reserved for shadows. Squinting in the honeyed light, I saw that even transitory visitors must accept its Midas touch, surrendering their secret selves entirely to its golden sheen. I drove on.

The West awed me. Without warning, the Rocky Mountains split the gauzy clouds. Their august omnipresence reigned in all directions. The haze, in royal purple, unfolded at their bases. The highway unscrolled more like imperial summons than mere road. On either side, canyon walls, plummeting to rivers or rising toward heaven, demanded both my homage and my will to choose. They stood as silent sentinels, blocking divergent thought or spontaneous explorations.

For loyal subjects in its realm revere "the land." Their adoration for the mountains fell like fringe down their vests and flashed like silver buckles on their heritage. They talked ceaselessly in boldface capitals about "the land." They talked about loving "the land." They talked about preserving "the land." They talked about protecting "the land" from the uncaring. They talked about hardships living on "the land," as if their perseverance were precious metal only they could mine. They even talked about talking about "the land."

After a few days, their ever-present proclamations pinched. Like inlaid boots bought for Saturday night show, their unrelenting articulations, however sincere, were just too stiff and tight for me. I began to long for home.

I learned I loved the Ozarks as I drove back east. With the mountains' steep angles diminishing and the yellow plains, a straight-line blur, behind me, I drove back to the Plateau. I liked the gentle, steady rise of its slopes. Traveling on top, the land neither obliterated me in it nor obligated me to it. The hills rose and fell in long, slow, deep breaths. Their rhythm eased my weary nerves. Gnarled and knuckled limestone lay like work-worn hands, folded quietly in welcome. Chicory, black-eyed Susans, trumpet creepers, ox eye daisies, and goldenrod nodded quiet invitations to butterflies and passersby. Their blue and orange and white and yellow beckoned, bite size appetizers from the color buffet. Sycamores with bony fingers pointed to crooked streams that cut and cornered fields. In the tangle of blackjack groves, around twisted gravel paths, sanctuary and intrigue awaited. If I chose to turn off the interstate, I could sample either.

The Plateau waters did not splatter from loud and cascading waterfalls, but grew by droplets deep within the Ozark earth. Spring-fed and forest-filtered, they flowed flat, wide, and clear. Fishermen, chest-deep in wordless sport, broke the glassy surface. But downstream, the current smoothed silver again. The quiet seeped into my dry places. When I returned to the Plateau's conversations, I was glad. In their easy words, I discovered Ozarkers love the land from their shoes up. Their soles wear from the edges out, and their toes are scuffed. Each day slips into a comfortable fit, soaked and softened by a lifetime's perspiration. Like long and leather laces, their talk strung loosely through cutting wood, picking tomatoes, weeding gardens, and peeling apples. Their weekend entertainment crisscrossed the county fair, float trips, and showing horses. Their unspoken devotion tied each syllable to the terrain.

I came to love the Ozarks when I left it. The land did not claim me; I claimed it. And to be nourished, I came home again.

Lizabeth Cox

Appendix

If You Can't Get Here from There

The following addresses, telephone numbers are provided for first-person contact with these stars of the Ozarks.

The Lights of Branson

Baldknobbers Jamboree
P. O. Box 972
Branson, Missouri 65615
417-334-4528
www.baldknobbers.com

Jennifer's Americana Theater
P. O. Box 1987
Branson, Missouri 65615
417-33-Jennifer (417-335-3664)
jennifer@tri-lakes.net

Ride the Ducks
P.O. Box 1837
Branson, Missouri 65615
417-334-3825

Shepherd Hills Factory Outlets
Branson: Factory Merchant's Outlet Mall
1000 Pat Nash Drive
Headquarters: Exit 127 off I-44 Lebanon
1-800-727-4643
417-532-7000

Kanakuk-Kanakomo Kamps
Spike and Darnell White
1353 Lakeshore Drive
Branson, Missouri 65616-9470
417-334-2432

The Lights of Ozark and Douglas Counties

Dawt Mill
HC 1 Box 1090
Tecumseh, Missouri 65760
417-284-3540

Zanoni Mill
Dave and Mary Morrison
HC 78, Box 1010
Zanoni, Missouri 65784
417-679-4050
bbim.org/zanoni

Hodgson Mill
Box 5
Sycamore, Missouri 65760

Edwards Mill
College of the Ozarks
Branson, Missouri
417-334-6411, ext. 3354

Rockbridge Mill and Trout Farm Restaurant
P.O. Box 100
Highway N, Road 142
Rockbridge, Missouri 65741
417-679-3619
rtr@webound.com
www.rockbridgemo.com

Assumption Abbey
R.R. 5
Box 1056
Ava, Missouri 65608
417-683-2258
aabakery@yahoo.com

Laura Ingalls Wilder Home and Museum
3068 Highway A
Mansfield, Missouri 65704
417-924-3626
liwhome@windo.mo.org

Woodpro Cabinetry, Inc.
P. O. Box 70
330 Walnut
Cabool, Missouri 65689
1-888-296-6377

The Lights of Marshfield and Conway

The Dickey House
331 South Clay Street
Marshfield, Missouri 65706
417-468-3000

Richard and Judy Kerb
Den of Metal Arts
P. O. Box 126
Conway, Missouri 65632
417-589-8326

The Lights of Buffalo, Bennett Spring and Nevada

Hale Fireworks
N Highway 65
Buffalo, Missouri
417-345-7758

Bennett Spring State Park
26248 Highway 64
Lebanon, Missouri 65536
Cabin Reservations 417-532-4307
Dining Lodge 417-532-4547
Swimming Pool 417-588-2071

Charlie Reading's Fly Shop
11937 Highway 64
Lebanon, Missouri 65536
417-588-4334

Carolyn Gray Thornton
Route 4, P.O. Box 94A
Nevada, Missouri
cgthornton@u-n-i.net

Ellen Gray Massey
125 Maple Drive
Lebanon, Missouri 65536
417-532-5155
egm001@llion.org

Hillbilly Days
Lebanon Area Chamber of Commerce
500 East Elm Street
Lebanon, Missouri 65536
417-588-3256

The Lights of Lebanon

Jim Bohannon
Westwood One Radio
1755 South Jefferson Davis Highway
Arlington, Virginia 22202

Barry McKenzie
26163 Pecos Drive
Lebanon, Missouri 65536
417-532-8434

Independent Stave Company
Barrels of Fun
1078 South Jefferson
Lebanon, Missouri 65536
417-532-7700

Eric Tudor
459 North Madison Street
Lebanon, Missouri 65536
417-588-9523
RRIVERWIND@aol.com

The Lights of Richland, Fort Leonard Wood, Steelville, and Jefferson City

Nancy Ballhagen's Puzzles
25211 Garden Crest Road
Lebanon, Missouri 65536
417-286-3837
www.odd.net/ozarks/puzzle

Caveman Bar-B-Q and Steak House
26880 Rochester Road
Richland, Missouri
573-765-4554

U.S.Army Engineer Museum
573-596-0780
Fort Leonard Wood, Missouri 65473

Ethel Hickey
60 Blunt Road
Steelville, Missouri 65565
573-786-8102

Jim Widner
1427 Briar Village Court
Jefferson City, Missouri 65109

Bob Priddy
Missouri-Net
505 Hobbs Street
Jefferson City, Missouri 65109
800-669-7200

BIBLIOGRAPHY

Rising Star and Ozark Constellations stories were selected from the four hundred features Vicki Cox has published. They originally appeared in the following publications:

Appaloosa Journal

Branson Living Magazine

Grit Magazine

Mobile (AL) Register

The Ozarks Mountaineer

The Ozarks Senior Living Magazine

Rural Arkansas

Rural Missouri

St. Louis Globe Democrat

St. Louis Post-Dispatch

School and Community Magazine

Springfield! Magazine

Springfield News-Leader

Today's Woman

INDEX